Highland, Lowland and Island

Highland, Lowland and Island

Three Long-Distance Walks in Scotland

ROGER LEGG

Rev. date: 02/02/2016

To order additional copies of this book, contact:
Xlibris
800-056-3182
www.Xlibrispublishing.co.uk
Orders@Xlibrispublishing.co.uk
727296

To my grandchildren
Matthew, Oliver, Eleanor
Thirza, Simon and Katie
with love and affection

From the lone shieling of the island
Mountains divide us, and the waste of seas —
Yet still the blood is strong, the heart is Highland,
And we in dreams behold the Hebrides.
Canadian Boat Song

CONTENTS

LIST OF MAPS

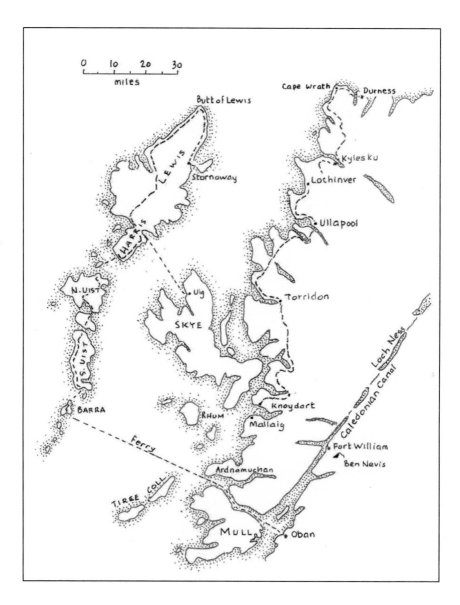

Overall routes (1) Cape Wrath to Knoydart (3) The Outer Hebrides

FOREWORD

Cape Wrath to Knoydart

In *Another Shore* I wrote about six long-distance walks that I had made in the British Isles from 1980 to 1991. One of these journeys was the length of Scotland from Allendale Town to Durness in 1982; I had hoped to finish my journey at Cape Wrath though, as I recorded:

> I made my way to Keoldale, though from what I had been told the previous day it was doubtful whether the ferry would be running. But, there it was, getting ready to leave with a young couple, complete with bicycles mysteriously hired from somebody who wasn't in town (as I had been informed the previous day). The ferry was not what I had expected – a dinghy with an outboard motor, and looking inadequate for a choppy sea. The ferryman told me that because of the tides he would not be able to bring me across on the return journey and that I would then have to walk out around the head of the Kyle. This would mean another eight miles on top of the twenty-six from the ferry landing to the Cape and back, more than I cared to walk in a day; there were other explorations that I could make without making walking a penance.

So I returned a year later and walked to Cape Wrath, continuing down the west coast to Knoydart, a route said by many to have the finest coast in Britain.

Galloway to Iona

The walk from the Rhinns of Galloway to Iona was an attempt to complement that from Cape Wrath to Knoydart, to explore the length of Scotland's western coast. There were many attractions in a route along the south-west coast, starting at the most southerly point in Scotland and finishing in Iona, a place of pilgrimage for centuries. The missing 'gap' between the two routes was Ardnamurchan, an area I had visited on my coast-to-coast walk across Scotland in 1981.

The Outer Hebrides

Anyone studying the map of Britain cannot fail to be attracted to the string of islands that make up the Outer Hebrides. They lie like a defensive barrier for the north Scottish mainland, against the mighty waves of the Atlantic Ocean. Many visitors have written of the great beauty, the quality of the light, the hospitality, the peace and quiet. For the long-distance walker there is the attraction of a route of about 150 miles, from Barra to the Butt of Lewis, across a variety of terrain, a number of ferry crossings, and a continuous route open only to the cyclist and pedestrian. The connection between the other two journeys recorded in this book is only the thread of time and the expedition which ended in Iona. And there, on my last morning, I had looked out over the sea to those distant shores on the horizon and said to myself, "One day, God willing, I'll go there." And so in 1987 I made a two-week journey to the Western Isles.[1]

---

[1]   *The Hebridean Way*, Scotland's latest long-distance footpath, is due to be officially opened in 2016. The route follows much of the way that I have described in my expedition.

- 1 -

Cape Wrath to Knoydart

The days before setting off for Durness, were more hectic than usual. On Thursday and Friday I had assembled the pages of my PhD thesis and taken them to the binders. After seven years research work I felt somewhat like Bunyan's Pilgrim when he lost the load from his back. On Saturday we went down to Steyning to celebrate my mother's 80th birthday, a glorious day of sunshine with nearly thirty members of the family gathered together, sons and daughters, grandchildren, great-grandchildren, brothers, sisters, nephews and nieces. On Sunday, after the morning's service in Bromley, I took my daughter Ruth to Paddington to start her midwifery course at St Mary's Hospital; her room in the nurses' home was on the fourth floor and, in the sweltering heat we had to make several portages of gear up seemingly endless stairs and through narrow corridors – no doubt good training for my trip. Then, that evening, I caught the train to Scotland to fulfil my resolve of walking to Cape Wrath and then by devious ways along the north-west coast, to Knoydart.

Monday 3rd September, return to Durness
The Nightrider from Euston to Glasgow was a relatively inexpensive way to get to Scotland (£19 single) costing about half the normal fare, with the added bonus of first-class accommodation and taking only six and a half hours for the journey though, in spite of the smooth ride, I didn't get much sleep. Also railway stations at 6-o'clock in the morning

are not the most scintillating of places at which to arrive. However, at Queen Street station I had an enjoyable conversation with a Bristol lad, an undergraduate at Portsmouth Polytechnic. He saw me studying my O.S. map in the breakfast bar and wanted to know whether I was a geologist; he was off to do some mapping near Oban as part of his geology course.

The train from Queen Street left at 7.35 a.m. and after making connections at Perth and Inverness, we arrived at Lairg soon after one o'clock. A bus was waiting in the station yard and following a scheduled break in the town we left for the north-west coast. I sat next to a 73-year-old Yorkshireman who was visiting some of his old climbing haunts. He was a fund of information and full of enthusiasm for this part of the country. At the age of 60 he had been to Iceland with a trekking group and had carried a 40lb pack. A recent heart attack had left him unable to tackle mountains but he still loved travelling. Passing through the Achfary Estate he pointed out a telephone box, painted black in keeping with the rest of the Duke of Westminster's Estate.

The bus arrived in Durness three hours after leaving Lairg, having made deviations to small villages such as Scourie and Kinlochbervie. The youth hostel had been upgraded since the previous year, for better or worse I don't know. It was certainly more comfortable, though the old black, coal-fired stove, around which we had sat, yarned and warmed ourselves, had been removed.

Compared to London which was enjoying a heat wave, the weather was cold and breezy. However it wasn't raining so, after a meal, I went for a stroll to the Smoo caves and then by track into the hills to the pass by Beinn Ceannabeinne (a route which cuts off a fair amount of road around Loch Eriboll and one which I could well have followed the previous year). It was good to be out in solitary places so soon after leaving London but the five mile walk had left me worn-out and I wondered how I would cope with the longer distances that lay ahead of me – and with a 30lb pack.

Back at the hostel I rang Iris; Ruth had also phoned home rather distressed because we had left her pots and pans behind and she was now stuck without facilities for cooking. A number of lively people staying at the hostel, including an extrovert West Indian, from

Liverpool, now working in London – I was to meet him again farther south. Then there were two young Scotsmen who had climbed over 200 Munros, some several times according to their marked up copy of the 'Tables'. They were very quiet and it was hard to imagine them walking anywhere, let alone climbing a mountain; today they had been on Ben Hope.

Tuesday 4th September, Cape Wrath

I slept well and woke to a brilliant morning. Alan Harmer, an incomer working at the craft village, wrote poems about this beautiful land. One of his duplicated booklets lay open on the breakfast table, with a message of anticipation:

> *Never before have I looked so lovingly*
> *at the land around me,*
> *And loved it more.*

On leaving the hostel at 9.30, I bought enough food for the two day walk around the Cape Wrath peninsular and then went down to the craft village at Balnakeil, the various units of which advertised the usual assortment of craft goods, chess sets, pottery, needlework and cuddly toys. Possibly the most unusual unit was the Boss boatyard which had built John Ridgeway's boat *Debenhams*, but I could see nothing advertised about this business. As a boatyard it is unusual in the sense that it was many miles from a harbour. When Alan Boss had the contract for Ridgeway's boat he did the work in Southampton and then sailed round the world with her in the 1977/78 Whitbread Race.[2]

At Balnakeil Farm I met John, the church warden, out with his dog. He had recently retired as the farm manager but, though 79 years old, he still worked around the farm – he was now doing some fencing. The previous year his church had been without an organist and he was pleased to tell me that recently the local school teacher had agreed to play for them.

---

[2] The *Debenhams* came 13th out of 15 boats in the race. Farther down the coast, at Ardmore, is the Adventure School that John Ridgeway set up about 40 years ago; the school is now run by his daughter Rebecca.

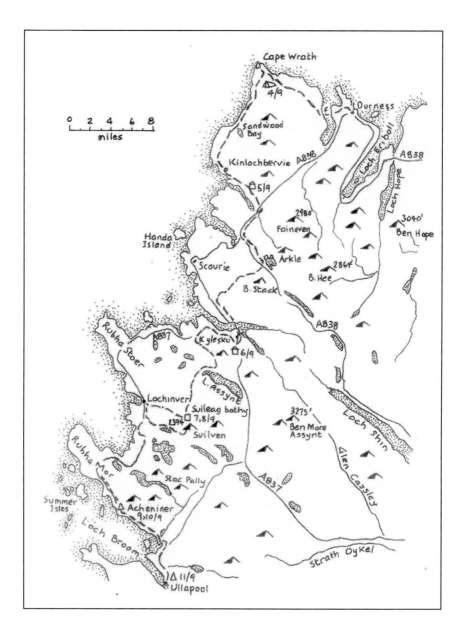

Durness to Ullapool

After looking in at the churchyard to see the chieftain's grave,[3] I cut across country by an unmapped footpath which John had told me about ("Ye'll see yon wicket gate."), by the old school by Loch Caladail, a mile or so away from the road. I walked fast to be in time for the ferry at Keoldale but I could have relaxed as it was making at least three trips to get some twenty people across – I was at the end of the queue. In front of me were two elderly couples from Sussex, full of fun but hardly dressed for an expedition to the Cape. Our turn came at last, the water was choppy and the waves broke over the bow; one of the windows had broken away from the cabin leaving a gaping hole so that the water sprayed into the boat and over the passengers. So casual, anything rougher and the boat could have floundered. The landing on the other shore was on a sand bank via upturned milk crates, not the best of places to alight, especially in high heels, but the Sussex folk took it all in good spirits.

From the ferry landing a mini-bus was available for the eleven miles of road to the Cape, and I was the only one who opted for shank's pony. The loaded bus didn't pass me until I had covered some two miles, and later in the day when it was empty, the driver stopped to offer me a lift. After Daill, where a Bailey bridge had replaced a ford, heavy rain brought out my waterproofs; the rain soon cleared and the remainder of the day was fine with good visibility and distant views. I had my lunch in a barn overlooking Loch Inshore, which is in the middle of the DANGER ZONE. At one time there had been nine productive sheep farms around here; today I saw no sheep at all and most of the farms in the area are deserted because of the bombing range.[4]

---

[3] See *Another Shore,* p153.

[4] In 2008 there had been a strong possibility that the land around the lighthouse would be part of the bombing range; local people and walkers feared that the MoD's ownership would lead to further restriction on the peninsula. However the MoD dropped its application and the local Durness Development Group will now have the first option to buy the land.

I left the road to drop down to one of these farms at Kearvaig, now a bothy maintained by the MBA,[5] in a delightful sheltered bay under Col Mor, at 850ft the highest sea cliff on the British mainland. I was tempted to camp there for the night but taking account of the next day's plans, I decided to carry on along the cliffs and over the moor to the lighthouse. On the way, for about a mile under Dunan Mor, stretched a large, well-made dry stone wall of granite, some stones of which must have weighed more than half-a-ton. Hamish Brown recorded in his *Groats End* book that: 'The keeper could tell me nothing of the wall – he had not even walked up the hill.' The keeper I met today was friendly and informative about the lighthouse and its associated buildings which were in the process of a major renovation, most of the materials for which were delivered by helicopter. The builders and electricians engaged in the work had been living there throughout the summer months, with occasional weekend breaks.

As well as their primary duties of looking after the light, fog signal and radio beacon, the keepers did most of the maintenance work on the station, some deliveries by helicopter and major deliveries, once or

---

5   MBA: Mountain Bothy Association, a registered charity whose mission statement is: *to maintain simple shelters in remote country for the use and benefit of all who love wild and lonely places.* In 2013 there were about 100 bothies in their care.

twice a year, taken from a boat anchored off the Cape – only in severe weather was recourse made to the mini-bus. I climbed to the lantern via the lighthouse's 81 steps; the keeper told me something of what it is like in stormy weather but it didn't require much imagination to think what it would be like when a north-wester blows down from the Arctic –there is no land between here and the North Pole.[6]

I had forgotten to buy matches in Durness and the keeper kindly supplied me with a box, appealing greatly to my sense of humour – matches from a lighthouse. Then I walked back along the road to Clais Chamach, a defile which leads down to a small inlet where there is a jetty and oil storage tanks, camped by the stream and was in my sleeping bag by 8-o'clock. While cooking my evening meal I found that I had forgotten to bring a cup so that both soup and tea had to be drunk from an empty tin; years ago I would have been most upset about such an omission – but I had become rather more philosophical. After all, a tin does just as well as a mug.

---

[6] The lighthouse was built in 1828 by Robert Stevenson, the light shining for the first time on Christmas Day of the same year. It was converted to automatic status in 1998.

Wednesday 5th September, to Kinlochbervie

The morning was overcast, following overnight rain. After breakfast I was chased away by the midges which had become so numerous that I hastily packed my rucksack with my eyes shut and a towel wrapped around my face.

From the Cape the western coastline is initially rather tortuous, so I followed an inland moorland route for two miles or so before rejoining the coast at Keisgaig Bay. I spent some time at this remote place watching the sea birds before resuming my journey, now along an impressive line of cliffs. I dropped down to the sea at Strath Chailleach, anticipating a walk at sea level into Sandwood Bay,[7] but an incoming tide prevented this. Retracing my steps, I climbed over the headland to find myself in a 'slough of despond' from which I had to beat a hasty retreat. When the bay was finally reached, the sand wasn't firm enough for pleasant walking. On the other hand, the scenery lived up to expectations and one could trace the coastline to the lighthouse some eight miles away.

The bay has a number of legends. The most well-known is that of a local farmer, Alexander Gunn. A certain MacDonald Robertson often spoke of the time he met Alexander in 1939. This is what he said: "On 5th January 1900 ..... Gunn's collie suddenly let out a howl and cringed in terror at his feet. On a ledge, above the tide, a figure was reclining on the rock face. At first he thought it was a seal, then he saw the hair was reddish-yellow, the eyes greenish-blue and the body yellowish and about seven foot long. To the day Alexander died in 1944, his story never changed – that he had seen a mermaid of ravishing beauty."

From Sandwood Bay a path led to Loch a' Mhuilinn where I had a refreshing wash, some lunch and a snooze with my tent drying in the sun. Earlier, one or two showers had threatened a wet day but these soon cleared to give way fine weather. In the distance, explosions suggested that the RAF were engaged in target practice on their bombing range ten miles to the north-east. Perhaps I had been fortunate to have got through yesterday. When Hector Kyme started his long walk to Dover he had spent several days at Durness waiting to get to the

---

[7] Sandwood Bay is part of the Sandwood Estate run by the John Muir Trust.

Cape, because of the bombing. A number of others have had similar experiences, though today there is even a charity marathon to the Cape.

Two or three cars were using the track from Sandwood Loch to Blairmore that day – and here the scenery changed from the bleak green browns of moorland to grass and grey-white stones of all shapes and sizes. There were some trees in a garden here, the first I had seen for three days, which gave me great pleasure. Imagine living in a desert for months and then seeing trees for the first time – no wonder travellers get worked up about such things. Coming from the deserted land of Wrath the area seemed well-populated and relatively prosperous. I was told that Kinlochbervie was the fourth largest port in Scotland and also that it has the largest ice plant for fish on the north-west coast. The road from here to the A838 had been upgraded to two lanes to take the increase in lorry traffic resulting from this plant.

I called in at the New Inn for a pot of tea and nourishing sandwiches. It would have been a good place to stay but as I wanted to press on to shorten the next day's planned mileage, Mrs Morison kindly phoned Mrs White at Achresgill to check whether she had accommodation. Then, having climbed the hill out of the village, an outstanding view opened up of Loch Inchard, moor and mountains. Foinhaven had some cloud but Arkle and Ben Stack were clear. The Duchess of Westminster had three horses named after these mountains, one of which became the well-known and most popular of all steeplechasers.

Mrs White, who had lived here all her life, understood Gaelic but couldn't speak it, although her accent was so strong that when speaking to her friends she sounded as if she could! Her husband, who did speak the language, said that only older folk around there then used it.

Thursday 6th September, to Kylesku
Breakfast at 8.30 and I was on the way soon after nine on a brilliant morning before the sky rapidly clouded over though the rain that had been forecast failed to materialise.

About six miles of road brought me to Haxford Bridge. Halfway, a man was in the process of lifting out some peat from his patch on the high moor; by the look of the ground there was enough to last for generations. From the bridge I followed the footpath along the north side of the river which joins Lochs Stack and Laxford. There were several fishermen; at one point the river was crossed by a wire along which a basket could be pulled on a pulley, an odd contraption for the benefit of getting fishermen from one side to the other. From a footbridge over the river near Lochstack Lodge, a well-made stalkers path goes south-west for about six miles across some convoluted country with many streams, lochans. and low hills, which, apart from Ben Stack, are no more than 1000ft high. I would not have liked to have crossed this area without the aid of a path. The one I was on was a real pleasure, snaking out across the jumbled landscape, remote from any habitation. Coming out of this wild country, I lay down to rest, closed my eyes and the melody of quiet sounds, the tinkling brook and the rustling movements of the grass became a joyous symphony.

The path joined a road near Duartmore Bridge where there was a fish farm. Three miles of tarmac brought me to the new Kylesku Bridge, an uncompromising structure which looked out of place against the wildness of this country. It had recently been opened by the Queen (in 1984). Thus possibly the last obstacle of the car had been removed around the north-west of Scotland; the redundant ferry was out in the Loch, awaiting a buyer. In an attempt to offset the financial losses resulting from the closure of the ferry, Kylesku Village had had a grant from the EEC to promote its attractions – roadside notices advertised *Hotel, Shop, Fishing*. The new shop proved to be a motorised caravan though the hotel looked substantial enough. One couldn't complain about the scenery, which was beyond compare, with Quinag dominating the skyline to the south, while from the north to the east, the lochs and the lower hills glowed red in the setting sun. I found difficulty in keeping my finger off the camera. At ten o'clock the moon was rising from behind a hill; for some time the glow in the sky could be seen gradually growing brighter as I waited for its appearance. The first sight came as a silver streak on the edge of the hill's silhouette, blinding in its intensity; the fully risen moon seemed pale by comparison.

I found B&B accommodation with the lady who ran the old shop – she seemed to run most things in the village. I phoned Iris who told me that it was very cold in London – especially noticeable after all the recent warm weather.

Friday 7ʰ September, to Suileag

When planning my route at home I had thought of visiting Eas a' Chual Allinn, the highest waterfall in the UK, lying some miles off the road to the east of Unapool. Another priority of the trip was to climb Suilven which was to the south-west. With armchair travel it is easy enough to walk from place to place; the reality often requires a compromise and to take a more direct line. So I opted to head for Suilven, involving a zig-zag route of roads and paths. As it turned out it was a reasonable decision, for the day's weather brought low cloud, drizzle and heavy rain.

Breakfast was a substantial meal, not unexpected in these parts. A Belgian couple were also staying overnight, enjoying a motoring holiday through Scotland and returning via Newcastle where they had some friends from WWII. Soldiers had been billeted with them when the country had been freed from German occupation and they maintained their English friendships through their children. They told me that food had become quite plentiful in Belgium several years before UK rationing[8] ended and of how they had sent food parcels to their English friends.

Unapool was a disappointment – the name had appealed to me. On the other hand the coast road (B869) was as scenic as I had

---

8   Rationing after WWI didn't end completely until July 1954. Sweet rationing
     ended in February 1953, sugar in September of the same year; and meat was the
     last to become freely available again in 1954.

expected, six miles of twists and turns and gradients as steep as any road in the land, through a tortuous landscape enlivened by some splendid trees. Perhaps twenty cars passed me during two hours; about a mile from where I left the road for a footpath, the occupants of a superior Range-Rover offered me a lift.

The footpath through Gleann Leireaq doubled back under the western flank of Quinag, though I could see little of the cliffs because of the swirling mist. Loch an Leothaid was joined to Loch Vidhe na h-Larne by a pretty waterfall near where I met three OAPs who had walked up to the pass and were now returning. The climax of the path was the pass Bealach Leireig, under steep cliffs, and then a graded descent to Tumore by the road on the shore of Loch Assynt.

Two miles brought me to the end of the loch and to another path leading into Assynt Estate and to Suileag. According to a notice on the bothy door this was officially closed for the stalking season between 1st August and 21st October. In spite of all the open country surrounding the hut, I could find nowhere suitable to pitch my tent. The grass was too long and tusky so, taking a chance against keepers arriving and throwing me out, I went in, grateful for the shelter on a wild night with driving rain. I was also fortunate that the bothy had been renovated that year by the MBA, the work funded from a legacy by Percy Gray (1916-1983) and a grant from the Countryside Commission. Permission to use the shelter was by courtesy of the Assynt Estate. A generous supply of candles provided light, hundreds of tea bags left behind by the work parties gave me free brews and I was able to hang my wet clothes over the various ropes strung below the roof. The whole place was clean and tidy, although the sleeping platform of floorboards made for a hard bed. The last entry in the bothy book was dated 31st August by a party also grateful to find shelter from the rain, expressing delight in the building's state of repair.

Saturday 8th September, Suilven
I woke several times during the night because of the hard boards, the barking of deer (or otter), with the bothy grunting and groaning as the wind gusted against the roof. I was up at 6.45, freshening up with a wash in the stream, the early morning fine though overcast with the sun

trying to break through. The long northern flank of Suilven was clear at first but soon the cloud level dropped to hide this celebrated ridge.

It took me a long time to get going, a reluctance to don wet clothes. As I planned to stay another night, I tidied all the gear into one area of the hut to give the impression that I wasn't really in occupation! When at length I went outside it was raining cats and dogs, so I beat a hasty retreat into the hut – it didn't take much to put me off. Twenty minutes later the rain had stopped and I began again.

The walk to the flank of Suilven was trouble-free – fortunately I missed the principal path which turned out to be a quagmire. A strange and prominent feature, running in a straight line down the side of the hill was a large dyke on each side of which was a wall of scree. It could have been man-made, but why? The climb to the Bealach Mor, the saddle between the two principal summits, was steep and uneventful but along the summit ridge in the cloud, I felt rather apprehensive. There is a wall across this ridge but the walker is able to go through a gap which once boasted a gate. Sheep still roam along the top, and also rabbits. From the flat-domed summit, only a comprehensive view of mist was revealed. I returned to the bealach and descended the south facing gully, taking it slowly, bit by bit, to reach the relatively level ground above which the mountain rises. Three miles of rough walking brought me round to the head of Fionn Loch to a well-made path high above the River Kirkaig and its wooded valley, leading to the sea loch of the same name.

A long twisting road, passing through three hamlets in as many miles, brought me to Lochinver. After years of studying the name on the map, the town proved a little disappointing; there were one or two traditional Scottish buildings but the others could have come from any town. It was also a long walk from one end to the other before I found a café, its doors closed so that it could accommodate a coach party. When it reopened, the food seemed so expensive that I resisted the temptation to buy anything except a pot of tea, despite the fact that I'd only had a bar of chocolate since breakfast – my lunch was still in the rucksack.

On the road out of town I found the garage of a house open – a very tidy garage – so I took possession to have a belated lunch. Just as I was starting to eat, the car came back. The lady driver was pleasant and understanding, not at all embarrassed to find a strange man in there; in fact she invited me to have a cup of tea which I politely declined in view of my recent café stop.

Farther along the road, at Glen Canisp Lodge, a notice at the gate warned people not go into the Assynt Forest between August 1st and October 21st due to the possibility of being shot at (being mistaken, I suppose, for deer).

NOT ICE

Visitors are asked not to go over the forest after
August 1st and are warned that it may be dangerous
to do so after that date because of rifle fire.

I read this notice as Not Ice, not spotting a gap between the 'not' and 'ice', before I realised what the word was. On reflection, perhaps room had been left to insert another 'n'.

The last four and a half miles of the day seemed a long way and the sight of the bothy was most welcome; my pleasure doubled when I found that an eviction order hadn't been served and that my gear was intact. With the rain and wind beating on the roof, it was good to be 'home' again.

Sunday 9th September, to Achiniver
Another fitful sleep with vivid dreams, no doubt encouraged by the hard boards. I left soon after ten for the walk back into Lochinver in order to attend morning service which started at mid-day. This was a happy, well-attended occasion led by an archetypal Church of Scotland minister, though this impression may have been solely due to his accent. He had a lively talk for the children of whom there were about twenty – all seemingly with bright mischievous eyes. On the wall of this church was a memorial:

Erected

by the congregation and friends

in grateful memory of

JAMES GORDAN

who died 16th March 1926 aged 72

He was for 50 years a devoted

member and elder of

this church

which by his zeal and enterprise

was removed stone by stone from Naim

and re-erected on its present

site in 1903

Sadly, the minister told me that there was nothing written about this tremendous undertaking or of the faith of the man who caused it to happen.

After the service there was a fortnightly church dinner, announced as *Just a plate of soup, bread and tea*, but this turned out to be a far more lavish affair – at least for a hungry walker – with plenty of cheese, butter for the bread and home-made cakes. Yesterday's lady-of-the-garage was serving some of the food; naturally I said, "Hello ... again." Then the minister said: "You know who that is; that's my wife!" Much laughter. Sitting next to me were a retired couple from England (London and Lancashire). He had been a master craftsman for many years, a machinist with Rolls Royce and they had spent many walking holidays here, having fallen in love with the area. The lady organist, mother of two mischievous boys, was a teacher at one of the local single-class primary schools (there were three in the area and she had five pupils); each one of the schools had a micro-computer; Lochinver may be remote but they certainly moved with the times.

The dinner was well attended and at least ten visitors came along, mostly youngsters from overseas. I was pressed to take sandwiches and cake for my journey. This recommended in the car of the church warden, Francis Wayne and his wife Joan, whose bungalow home was situated in an unrivalled setting on a wooded promontory by Loch an Eisg-brachaidh.

They dropped me outside their house, where I changed back to my walking clothes, using the rack of a fisherman's van as a clothes rack – when the fisherman came back to load his catch into the van there he was none too pleased with my initiative (natives are not always friendly).

From here there followed three hours of road walking across Inverpolly Forest, the road twisting and turning through a contorted landscape. As I was heading into squally rain round the head of Loch Usgaig, the Range-Rover of a few days ago pulled up and the couple offered me another lift, an offer I did not refuse; sometimes principles have to give way to common courtesy. Though very well-to-do, with all sorts of up-market gear, this couple were so friendly and helpful, taking me to the end of the road which led to the youth hostel at Achininver.

The hostel, a converted croft reached by a footpath, was remote from other houses and had no electricity, no telephone, heating by an old coal stove and lighting by Tilly lamp. The bedroom for men, built into the roof space, held 28 beds. The women were downstairs with ten beds; viewed from the outside, the building seemed far too small for all this accommodation. The outlook over Loch Broom can only be described as perfect with Horse Island a mile offshore and the evocative Summer Isles further to the west.[9] The spiky mountains of Coigach rose dramatically behind the hostel. The warden was an OAP from Edinburgh who had been here for the previous 17 seasons, one of the longest serving wardens in Scotland. Though rather dour, he had some good stories and knowledge of the locality. The whole of this peninsula is known as Rubha Coigach. In the old days, not so many years ago, the laird would come back to his estate by horse carriage; the horses left at the estate boundary and, out of respect for him, the men would pull the carriage! This laird finally fell on hard times. He had refused to increase the rents in line with inflation and the estate had to be sold to pay off the debts. Today, most of the land is common grazing, run by a committee of independent crofters.

Out in the loch was a fleet of factory ships and trawlers, at night, fairy-like with glittering lights. The reality was hard work and big business, Scottish trawlers supplying Russian and East German factory ships with up to one and a half million tons of mackerel; my mind boggled at the thought of the number of creatures required to make up

---

[9] See End Notes.

that amount of fish. The whole operation was supervised by a single UK fishery protection vessel to ensure that annual quotas were adhered to.

Monday 10th September, Ben Mor Coigach

I decided to stay put for a day, explore the locality and investigate the Rock Path which leads along the coast to Ullapool – I had been warned that it was difficult to follow in bad weather. But first there was the daily 'task' to be completed and this entailed some back-breaking work, taking barrow loads of earth and stones to make up part of a worn stretch of footpath leading to the hostel. I was none too keen about this as it prevented an early start – but our warden was a taskmaster, not to be brooked; old he might have been but still a tough wee Scot. Finally he declared he was satisfied with our performance and I was able to get away at 10.30.

Along the coast the path passes the deserted croft of Achnacarinan (meaning a fish-net) reflecting the fishing along this coastline. Salmon have been caught for generations, the fish swimming between the mainland and the Summer Isles. The path worked its way under the cliffs of Carbh Choineacharn until Geoaha Mor where the stream Barbh Allt runs into the sea. As I missed the path which drops down to the stream (viewed from high up this didn't seem favourable), I followed it for two miles using a sketchy path before climbing the steep heather, grass and rock slopes onto Ben Mor Coigach (2500ft). From the summit there were good views along yesterday's coastline and of Stac Polly whose outline had the shape of the Pipes-of-Pan. Having reached the top I had ambitions of traversing some of the other ridges, but as I started again the cloud level dropped and when a cold rain storm hit me, I decided to take the short route to the hostel, arriving at 4.30, tired and hungry having had little to eat since the morning. However, after a rest I was ready for more action, completing a hostel task by bringing down a barrow load of coal from the pile which had been dumped that morning by the roadside, 600 yards away; then an invigorating bathe in the stream before settling down to a meal of scrambled eggs which Dave had kindly bought for me in the village. Dave was an Irishman who had come here on his motorbike and was staying for a week; he had been on holiday here several times and loved the solitude and tranquillity of the place.

An old lady had also come to stay for the night. Today she had walked most of the way from Lochinver with a small pack, having previously left most of her gear at Achmelvich Hostel. She brought one or two messages from a number of the warden's friends. Then two young women came in. A pretty German girl had fallen in love with the smaller Scottish hostels, wanted to see Achininver and she had been driven here from Ullapool by an English girl. The warden shed his dourness when they arrived but his new-found cheerfulness didn't last long – after about an hour the two girls decided to return to Ullapool as the German felt ill with a heavy cold.

The warden, who liked to travel during his time away from the hostel, told us how he had made a short visit to London earlier this year. He had wanted to get into the Houses of Parliament, to the Speaker's Gallery. As there had been a long queue and he hadn't the time (or patience?) to wait for his turn, he slipped in behind the group of eight people who were being admitted. At the final security check, to avoid showing his non-existent pass, he was able to point out a bag that someone had just put down, thus diverting the officer's attention (!) and enabling him to achieve his objective, illustrating both the resourcefulness of an archetypal Scotsman and the relative insecurity of the parliamentary buildings.

Tuesday 11th September, to Ullapool

Having forestalled the warden's road building plans by last night's coal delivery, I was able to make a relatively early start. I had with me a route-finding sheet which the warden had prepared and, after retracing yesterday's steps, I was able to locate the path dropping down to the Carbh Allt. As the fording place looked far too dangerous I had to go down to the small pebbly beach and cross the stream by boulder hopping. Beyond this point there was enjoyable walking, some rock scrambling along the steep hillside and also plenty of squelching bog; without a doubt, rather than being named Rock Path, Bog Path would have been more appropriate. On an early 19th century map this was the only route between Ullapool and Achiltibuie. I also recall reading that many years ago the postman used this path to deliver mail.

On a fine sunny day it would have been pleasant to have taken one's time over such a varied route, but as the weather was cold and showery I kept going and it was three hours before I stopped for a rest near the end of the path, overlooking Isle Martin and Strath Kancaird. From here I tried a short cut to get to the main road, but couldn't find the bridge indicated on the map. I went back to the route suggested by the warden's notes and compounded my folly by trying another short cut which turned out to be more bog than path before finally scrambling onto the A835 leading to Ullapool, five miles away.

By Ardmain I met a girl from New Zealand, recently arrived in the UK for a two-year holiday. She was working on a camp and chalet site on the tongue of land stretching out towards Isle Martin. I was grateful for a rest in her temporary caravan home, especially as it provided shelter from a heavy shower and a welcome cup of tea. Farther along the road another young woman was returning from her cleaning job in town. She and her husband owned a yacht based at Ardmain, which could be chartered for holidays and from which they earned their living. Their boat was then out at sea on one of those cruises though, because of the weather, the first two days had been spent on the loch.

There was a long hill before Ullapool; the sudden view of the town was like a jewel by Loch Broom and the surrounding mountains, reward enough for the tiring climb. Farther down the hill, I caught up with three fishermen from Peterhead, out for an afternoon's stroll whilst waiting for their trawler to be put back into service after a winch had failed. Their boat had a total crew of twelve men and it was stationed here for the mackerel season, supplying the factory ships. Their boat had sailed to many other fishing grounds around the world. It turned out that these men were also fishermen of another sort; having left them they caught up with me and one with an open, smiling face asked me, out of the blue: "Do you know the Lord Jesus as your Saviour?" I think they were a surprised when I said, "Yes, I do," before having some further chat about the Faith. They belonged to a Pentecostal house group in their home town.

I enjoyed coming into the town, having been away from shops for a week and felt like buying all the food in sight. This reminded me of the time I took Mark and Ruth to North Wales for the first time. After four days camping 'in the wilds' we went to Caernarvon for the day. When Ruth, aged six, saw the brightly coloured fare in the shop windows she said, with great feeling, "I wish I had a bag of gold."

Outside the hostel crowds queued to sign-in for the night. This is a popular place for many young people who are doing the 'grand tour' of Scotland. I let out a yell as I recognised Ted, the guy from Liverpool whom I had met at the Durness Hostel. He had finished escorting two German girls on their journey and had now met up with a colleague from London, ready for another round of the sights and sounds of Scotland.

Wednesday 12th September, to Camusnagaul
The well-appointed hostel is situated with good views overlooking the busy harbour but this also meant a disturbed sleep from the noisy machines associated with the boats, throbbing through the night. The weather remained cool and showery though the clouds were high and the mountains visible.

After essential visits to the bank, post office and shops, I went down to the jetty for the ferry. When a fisherman told me that it had just left I was flabbergasted – fortunately it turned out it was the ferry to Stornoway! Trying to track down the ferry which goes to Allt na h' Airbhe on the south side of Loch Broom was like trying to find a needle in a haystack. After visiting the harbourmaster's office and asking everyone in sight, I eventually found the little boat, hidden amongst her bigger sisters. At last the ferryman arrived, a student from St Andrews on a holiday job. To board the boat he wanted me to jump eight feet from a greasy wooden beam on to a slippery deck. The risk of a dislocated knee was too great so, in the end, he moved alongside another boat. Having got me on board he took the boat off to another quay to load on bags of food for the hotel at Allt na h' Airbhe. My diary failed to record the time of arrival on the other shore but it must have been quite late in the morning.

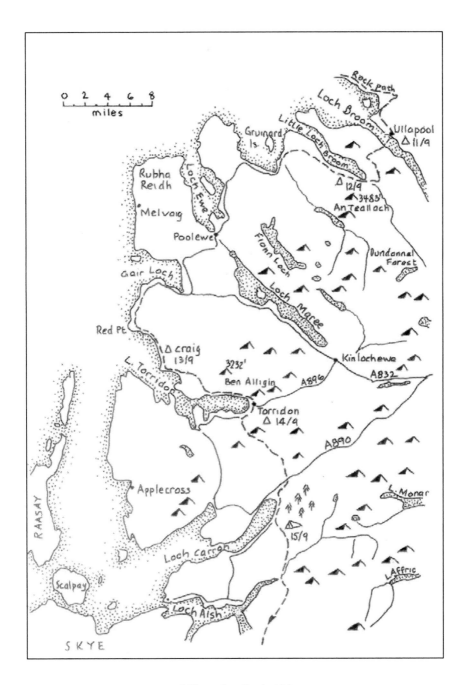

Ullapool to Loch Alsh

Moir, in his book of Scottish hill tracks, wrote that: "In bad weather the ferry may not operate." The alternative is a long journey of perhaps 20 miles around Loch Broom, if one wants to get to Dundonnel, as I did. When John Hillaby came this way from the south, his diary recorded:

> 13 June: Left Balharry in Dundonnell. Struck out for place on southwestern shore of Loch Broom where he thought I ought to be able to pick up ferry for Ullapool. Arrived at dusk. The cliff-tops, the last reputed breeding place of the sea-eagle, looked like the edge of the world. Immense vista, crinkly sea, toothy-looking rocks and islands in a Wagnerian sunset. Lights of what I took to be the very best Ullapool restaurants just visible on the opposite shore, but they might as well be a thousand miles away as there's no bloody ferry. Local Charon seems to have gone on strike with that pal of his in Totaig. May their bowels bust! And all those who have to do with marine transport. Place deserted. Bathed feet. Two more toenails missing. But still got six. Mooched about, looking for somewhere to sleep. Came across partly-constructed dream house of man who was building it for his ailing wife. Hospitably received by them both and crossed the loch next morning in boat carrying their workmen.

The trek across the neck of the peninsula was enjoyable but not strenuous. The farm land and woods of beech and oak in Strath Beaq were in complete contrast to all the wild country of the past days, an oasis in a region of remote and high mountains, dominated by An Teallach. Blackbirds were a joy to hear, as was the smell of pine trees coming down from the hills. A farmer was rounding up his sheep for a journey to Dingwall market the following day.

Dundonnel Hotel,[10] often mentioned in Scottish mountain books, proved far more superior than I had expected. Accommodation was

---

[10] At one time Dr Frank Fraser Darling lived at Dundonnell; here he began the studies which were to make him into a great naturalist and philosopher, publishing many books and scientific papers. He gave the 1969 Reith Lectures entitled *Wilderness and Plenty*.

expensive but the steak dinner was excellent and reasonably priced. I joined forces with a young postgraduate student from Dundee. It turned out that he had completed his PhD thesis on the same day that I had and, with a similar feeling of freedom, decided on a cycle tour of Scotland before leaving for the States where he had obtained a job with Xerox, researching silicon materials to replace semi-conductors. Peter had a faint accent which was hard to place; it turned out that his family was Dutch though he had received most of his education in Britain. He was rather disappointed that I had noted his accent. His professor was a world leader in his subject but, unable to obtain funds in this country for development work, received support from either the USA or Japan – an all too familiar story.

There was a possibility that Hamish Brown would join me here, to see me over An Teallach. As there was no news from him, I stayed at Sail Mhor, an independent hostel at Camusnagoul. Then, having some time and surplus energy on my hands, I went up into the hills; along a stream half a mile from the road there is an impressive waterfall running through an 80ft deep gorge which in some places is no more than six feet wide. I went on for a couple of miles behind the mountain of Sail Mhor but resisted the temptation to climb it with the excuse of having no emergency rations with me. This was just as well as by the time I had got back to the hostel, it was getting dark and the surplus energy had departed.

Independent hostels were then part of a new trend in accommodation available for people engaged in outdoor pursuits; there is more freedom and fewer rules than in a YHA hostel. The owner of Sail Mhor came here for the diving that Little Loch Broom offered, but he was now keener on climbing and guiding over An Teallach.

Thursday 13th September, to Craig

I had planned to walk through Dundonnell Forest by way of Shenavall bothy but the warden announced at breakfast that because of deer shooting activities, the bothy was locked. The route through to Kinlochure is one of the great walks in the Highlands through wild country, but on receiving this news I changed my mind and decided to go around the coast by way of Gairloch and stay at Craig, the remote hostel on the north west coast of Loch Torridon, having first checked that HB was not at the Dundonnel Hotel.

After six miles of walking in the rain along the coast road of Little Loch Broom, who should pass me but Ted and his friend in their car. He recognised me and naturally stopped – would I take a lift? I was unable to refuse. They were going to stay at Carn Dearg on the northern shore of Loch Gairloch but went out of their way by taking me to South Errodale. On the way we passed Gruinard Island, infamous because the ground has been poisoned with anthrax. Prominent notices on its perimeter forbid anyone to land.[11] We stopped at a hotel for a mid-morning cup of tea, served unenthusiastically by the manager, before going on past the celebrated Inverewe Gardens, and then lunching in a restaurant at Errodale. The Scottish landlord had been a policeman in London and on retirement he had bought the business. He told us something of the problems of this remote area, mostly financial. Local industry was now almost non-existent and the two resident fishing boats had been sold 'for a song'. Almost half the houses were up for sale and though most people here voted Conservative, they were disillusioned because the government showed no interest in supporting small industries. Outline planning permission for a road around the peninsula had been granted but there was no sign of final approval; if a road was built, that would have helped revitalise the area.

By the time we had finished our meal and conversation, the weather had cleared and I had a most enjoyable walk along the footpath to Craig with views of Skye, Raasay and the Applecross, peninsula across the loch. By Red Point there was an old fisherman's hut (the map indicated *Fishing Station*) now fallen into decay; there was springy grass turf, a joy to walk on, but soon this gave way to wet, stony and boggy terrain, back to the typical underfoot ground of this trip. Out on a small rock, a mile from shore, there was the mournful crying of sirens, seals or possibly mermaids.

The Craig youth hostel is situated about half a mile from the coast in a beautiful position, about half a mile from the shore. Up to the previous year, some of the surrounding land had grown crops, the last warden having run the place as a croft, now returning to nature.

---

[11] See End Notes.

Some supplies had to be delivered by boat, the coal for instance and a hostel task often means that the hosteller had to go down to the small bay with two buckets to collect it – I made one journey and found it hard work, carrying the coal uphill along an uncertain path. Some essential food was carried in by the warden from the Torridon road end, four miles away. Some renovation work had been going on during the summer, the building materials delivered by helicopter.[12]

Friday 14 September, to Torridon
The day began with a long lie-in, leisurely breakfast and a late start at half ten, then three miles of boggy path in wet and misty weather to join the road at Lower Diabaig. The crofter who looks after the hostel during the winter months kindly offered me a lift in his Land-Rover but I preferred shank's pony. The road had some steep hills, unkind to local cars, judged by laboured engine noises. At Torridon I popped into the small visitors centre, bought food at the post office-cum-store and booked into the modern youth hostel at 3.30 – possibly the shortest day 'on the road' of all my walking trips.

The hostel was crowded. I had long chats with several people: an unemployed Glaswegian, who had been on Liathach, but had failed to make the top in poor weather; a German woman and two sons, one of whom was entering the Lutheran ministry, were on a motoring holiday through Scotland and an unlikely couple, a Yugoslav married to a German girl. I expressed surprise that he should be over here (these were the days before the break-up of Yugoslavia) – he liked travelling and they were returning from a week in the Shetlands. Another was Dr Barton who had been camping by herself on Ben Alligan (two climbers I had met at Sail Mhor had met her on the mountain and been most impressed by her abilities) and had come into the hostel to dry out. Her husband was on the staff of Herriot Watt University and one of his pet projects involved an automatic weather station on the summit of Cairn Corm. She told me of the difficulties he had in raising the necessary finance; one would have expected that, among other interested parties, the skiing companies at Aviemore and the Met Office would have been

---

[12] Craig was closed down as a youth hostel some years ago; it is now a bothy maintained by the MBA.

only too keen to have sponsored this work. They had been on one of Hamish Brown's climbing trips to the west coast of Ireland and related how Hamish had insisted on porridge every morning (sounds like a man after my own heart) in spite of objections from the Bartons.

Later an Edinburgh school party came in, 30 enthusiastic boys and girls. I was cleaning up the kitchen for an evening task and in my most authoritative voice said: "Now guys, I don't want any mess – the kitchen's been cleaned." Immediate hush. "Anyone making a mess swims in the loch in the morning or takes a run up the mountain before breakfast." More hush. Dr Barton, who had been helping me clean up, was most impressed.

Saturday 15th September, to Torridon
I was up at seven attempting to beat the queue for the kitchen but many others had the same idea. The sun was breaking through revealing some of the mountains, promising a fine day as I left at nine o'clock, taking the road to the south shore of Loch Torridon in order to gain the tracks leading south. The path was easy to follow, stream crossings made relatively easy with stepping stone boulders, though some courage was needed to leap from one to the other, weighed down as I was by my pack. By Loch an Eion I unintentionally took a path on the south side of Maoe Cheamdearg, failing to check the map because of over-confidence in my route finding. Fortunately, this alternative route added little distance to the day's walking and I was rewarded by the sight of some immense silvery slabs of rock on An Ruadh-stac, which were not shown on the map. From here to a well-built but unnamed croft, boarded up with damaged doors and windows. After a long rest and snooze, I made my way down the valley with the weather improving all the time, the clouds lifting off the highest peaks.

On leaving the main road (A890), my route followed tracks along the River Carron to New Kelso, taking my chance across a field with a bull and a herd of cows. Fortunately he was content with his harem and not interested in me. A mile or so brought me to Strathcarron and the justly famous railway line between Dingwall and the Kyle of Lachalsh. I expected a café or two but unable to find one, I couldn't satisfy my longing for a pot of tea. The road gave a stiff climb with rewarding views over the Carron and across to the mountains through which I had come. Working my way behind Attadale House, a private road brought me to a grassy bank beside a bridge. It was still only late afternoon but it was unlikely that I would find a better camp site, so I pitched my tent there, had a good splash in the stream, a leisurely meal and retired to an early bed.

The fine weather was rapidly disappearing with winds and cloud building up out of the western sky. Someone who walked past with their dog didn't disturb me – by the time I looked out of the tent they were gone. Though I had been meeting people I felt rather lonely; the only animals here were some slugs, and I said to them with something like affection, "Hello, you lovely creatures."!

Sunday 16th September, to Shiel Bridge

It rained on and off all night and everything was damp on a grey morning; happily, apart from some condensation on the tent walls, it was reasonably dry inside the tent. Midges hovered outside the tent door but, unlike the slugs of the previous evening, I felt no friendliness towards *them*. I worked slowly through the jobs that needed to be done before the rain stopped in time for the final packing of tent and ground sheet.

A private forestry road brought me on to a well-made track by Carn Allt na Bradh, a nice wee hill of 1100ft, into Glen Ling. Though the mountains only rise to 2500ft above this glen, they seemed much more extensive than one might have expected from the map. Near Nonach Lodge at the head of Loch Long, one of the gardens contained pear and plum trees. A pleasant woman told me that the weather was mild in this locality and fruit can be grown satisfactorily.

From here I followed the road to Carnas-Cuinie, a hamlet of contrasting new houses, tumbled down shacks with thatched roofs and wrecks of cars in an old quarry; with a little more care the place could have been made very attractive. A steep climb along a FH&C path[13] brought me on to the main path going south crossing a col at 1500ft. This was another well-made path, though little wider than a sheep

---

[13] FH&C: a faith, hope and charity path, boldly defined on the map, hard to find on the ground; paths which start out bravely often either go off in the wrong direction or soon peter out. Consequently, one has to have *faith* to keep going, be *charitable to* the map makers and/or land owners and *hope* to come out at the place one is aiming for.

track, with cairns at a few awkward places for which, in the mist and heavy rain, I was grateful as the topography was somewhat confusing. The path finally rose to 1600ft before dropping down steeply into Coire Dhuirmid, a steep-sided valley with the An Loth Allt waterfalls, in one of whose 'cracks' were three large chock stones, each of which must have weighed many tons. Halfway down the valley I sheltered in a small corrugated iron hut – after five hours of walking I needed a rest and somewhere to eat my chocolate and shortbread.

The last of the day's walking belonged to the main road (A87) along Loch Duich, except for a brief excursion into the grounds of Inverinate House where I was challenged by a housekeeper but allowed to continue to gain a path by the shore. Everything was well maintained, much of the estate woodwork had been painted blue and even the motor boat had a canopy of the same colour. I was told later that the place was owned by an Arab chief who had recently brought in 40 guests by helicopter; they had departed only the previous day by the same means. Last week three sheep had been bought for a ritual festival and these had had to be carefully selected. As usual, the local people had mixed feelings about foreigners buying an estate – to some they brought much needed work and money, whilst to others they were very much outsiders. I thought, how much like a cross between an old highland chief and an absentee landlord.

At Invershiel a museum for the Clan Maciennan had recently opened – a rather primitive and ramshackle affair in an old stables. There were some interesting items with a curious mixture of Scottish and Red Indian artefacts. A family tree traced the clan back to the Kings of Ireland; the woman caretaker told me that some people had taken the 'tree' back to King David and Joseph of Arimathaea. Someone had also found a replica of Solomon's Temple in Scotland and had given a piece of the corner stone to the museum!

Around the head of the loch was an abundance of bird life, the most I saw on the whole trip. Buzzards perched on fence posts were being mobbed by immature gulls. Herons flapped lazily across the water and there were also chaffinches, oystercatchers and hooded crows. I reached Ratagan youth hostel at 5-o'clock, a well-built, well-situated building where I was made welcome by both the warden and other hostellers – a New Zealand girl made me a cup of tea. I played chess with a German, losing both games.

Loch Alsh to Mallaig

Monday 17th September, to Loch Hourn

Another grey morning though the mountains were clear, the water of the loch perfectly still and herons standing sentry-like on the shore. I was on my way by nine o'clock, taking a path through the forest to join the road to Glenelg and Skye, the old military road to Bernera Barracks which Johnson and Boswell had travelled many years ago on their Highland tour. It twisted and turned, rising to over 1000ft through the large area of forest which was serviced by Ratagan Village. There were many fine trees and some stands have been felled; to my mind there is nothing quite so depressing as ground which has been cleared of trees leaving nothing but stumps. The usual practice today is to re-plant soon after felling but there was little sign of activity in that direction.

After four miles I turned off the road at Braeside into Glen More, with well-ordered crofts and plenty of sheep on the hillside, perhaps the most I had seen on this west coast trip. I stopped for a brief while at Suardalan, a well-maintained MBA bothy with pleasant bedrooms upstairs, signing my name in the visitors' book, as passing through.

For a mile or so I followed a track which continues into Glen Beag where there are the best preserved brochs on the mainland. However, my route was to the south-east rather than the west; walkers miss many interesting sights by not deviating from their chosen route. Though there is a right-of-way up the glen to Bealach Aoidhdailean (1500ft) into Cleann Dubh Lochain, it is not shown on the map, no doubt because the boggy terrain failed to produce a permanent path. Electricity pylons had recently been built and the ground had been much scarred from tracked vehicles.

The cloud was down to about 3000ft, covering the highest peaks including the Saddle to the north; rain was in the air though no waterproofs were needed. After a rest on the col I had a fast walk/run down to the river leading into Arnisdale from where the route climbs upwards and then descends steeply through attractive woodlands to Kinlochhourn. This is a remote area with one road which twists for twenty tortuous miles from the A87 near Invergarry – an adventure for a motorist, never mind a walker. In fact several cars were parked at the road-end and those who had driven here were taking gentle strolls along the path on the south shore of the loch.

I met the local shepherd, a tall rangey fellow. He asked me whether I was one of the Herriot Watt group for whom he had been waiting a couple of days – he had been asked to take them through to Barrisdale bothy. I had to disappoint him but what are *days* in such a remote place; in town we worry if someone is ten minutes late. He was able to tell me of two or three camping places along the loch. I could have reached the bothy but I was in no hurry as I wanted to savour this path which has been described as one of the best walks in the whole of Scotland, having about it a Himalayan quality. So three miles farther on I found the green bank of machair the shepherd had recommended, the sort of place about which one often daydreams. I was able to use my stove outside the tent, while gazing at reflections in the silent mirror of the loch. The midges came later.

Tuesday 18th September, to Inverie

A leisurely breakfast outside the tent, the midges tolerating my presence, herons with lazy wing-beats flew up and down the loch, gliding into their fishing positions along the rocky shore. I was reluctant to leave this idyllic spot.

From the camp the path twisted and turned alongside the loch, sometimes climbing over headlands, for another four miles to Barrisdale. On the opposite shore at Caolasmoir were two crofts, now renovated as holiday homes, with access by sea or by mountain track. At Leach an Aiseig stood a remnant of an old pine forest, though sadly some of the trees were dying. At the end of the track is the ruin of an old church overlooking the western end of Loch Hourn where the loch widens to one and a half miles. From here one can see an emerald green patch of croft at Li; a writer and his wife had set up home there bringing some new life to the land. Each day they took their young daughter to school, two miles across the loch to Corran.

A light plane had flown past me; it is on its way to Skye, I thought, but no, it had landed in a field in Barrisdale. The landowner had arrived to talk with his young keeper about the plans he had for next year. In less than an hour he was on his way again, bumping across the field to take off into the wind before banking around the enclosing hills and flying off in the direction from whence he came. The keeper drove away in an old Ford car, in use for just two miles of road.

Two men from Herriot Watt were at the bothy, preparing a list of repairs that needed to be carried out. We had a good laugh about the team that were supposed to arrive – they were the team and familiar with the territory, coming here for club meets and especially for New Year parties. The bothy itself was quite a splendid affair with kitchen stove, bath, flushing loo and some beds with mattresses. Earlier in the day I had met a man from Grantham carrying a heavy pack. Although he had only been out for one day he was weary of his load (he was even carrying a full water bottle). He had stayed at the bothy last night, having walked from Inverie, complaining about the state of the path, and the amount of bog – little did he know what was in store for him if he took the route I had suggested, for he didn't seem to appreciate the scale of the mountains which were in front of him. The two from HW were also rather worried about this innocent abroad; on his first serious walking trip he had come to one of the most remote areas in Britain.

Eight more miles of path and track, over the pass of Mam Barrisdale (1476ft), brought me to Inverie. The scenery was magnificent all the way, with great mountains, cirques, valleys and sea. Near the summit of the pass the rain and wind came on; one of the HW men had said that it was always a drafty place; in winter they had sometimes been blown over and once the weather had been so bad they had to return to Inverie.

Fishermen were on Loch an Dubh-loch-in, at the end of which was all the paraphernalia of a fish farm which had closed down two years previously. The final mile to Inverie began with a climb of 250ft over the brow of a hill – not much, but as tiring as it was unexpected, a cruel joke after a long walk. But then the path dropped down through woods to the sea, as refreshing as a Surrey lane, with mature trees of every description, horse chestnut, sycamore, beech, oak, pine, birch and larch. The village had a well-stocked shop which was just about to close at three o'clock. Times are regulated by the estate, the factor ensuring that rules are kept. Having stocked up with more than enough food, I returned to the private hostel, run by the estate for the use of walkers and the occasional worker who arrived from the 'mainland' – the only way in, apart from walking, is by the post boat or by the Estate's landing craft.

The hostel was well appointed, clean and comfortable, good value for £5 a night. The warden was Mrs MacG...., who was also the postmistress. When I came in she was energetically cleaning the loos and showers and said bluntly, "Oh, God, not another one." But her bark was worse than her bite and after supper she invited me to her house, half a mile away and we spent the evening talking about local affairs. She was a Glasgow girl, trained to be a nurse before going to work for Lord Astor on Jura. There she married Mrs MacG.... who was then the head gamekeeper,

The estate had had a lot of publicity in the 1980s, the owner having planned to sell. The Army had sought to buy it as a training ground but there was such a fuss both locally and nationwide that the plan was shelved. The National Trust for Scotland, and an ad-hoc group headed by Chris Brasher, and various conservation people, had put forward proposals which finally disappeared into thin air. Now it appears a property developer had made an offer which has been accepted and the deal was to be ratified shortly. Local crofters had also tried to put their point of view, all of which finally came to naught – except that some of the more vocal residents had lost their jobs, shades of Highland clearances in the 19th century.[14]

I left this warm hospitable home, Mrs MacC.... offering to take me back to the hostel by car, but I said, "No, I'll be okay thanks," not realising how dark it was under the trees. I was tempted to return and

---

[14] See End Notes.

ask for that lift but couldn't see my way back! I had to feel my way along, walking by faith rather than by sight. Fortunately, some distant building lights gave some guidance. It is astonishing how rarely one is literally completely in the dark – and then thankful for the smallest light.

Wednesday 19th September, return to London
The only other person staying at the hostel was Bill from Dingwall. His accent was so broad as to be well nigh unintelligible. Two days ago he had brought a lorry over in the landing craft to deliver a load of asphalt for the local road, but because of the weather the lorry had to be left behind – he was going on holiday and someone else would have to return for the vehicle.

The gale that was blowing meant a rough crossing in the mail boat, a solid, well-found, converted fishing boat. The sea was so steep that boat was continuously rising and falling, smashing into the waves and though the passage to Mallaig lasts for less than an hour, it was not long before I was being sick over the side. To add to my discomfort I also became soaked to the skin by sea spray, hence quickly resolving not to become a deep-sea sailor. By the time we disembarked at least one passenger was feeling pretty miserable. The Skye ferry which docked shortly afterwards had also had a rough crossing, judging by the travel-weary holidaymakers arriving at the rail station. The train journey to Fort William was followed by a bus to Glasgow and what was left of my stomach revealed itself as we twisted and turned alongside Loch Lomond. The night-rider to London where, on a cold, grey, wet morning, people were on their way to work; commuter-man is a curious sub-species of homo-sapiens, grim, never a smile on his/ her face, or any conversation. As I stood at the bottom of an elevator watching the streams of commuters I was tempted to cry out at the top of my voice, "Wake up London."

- 2 -

Galloway to Iona

Friday 17th May, Mull of Galloway
To get to Stranraer I caught the mid-morning Northern Ireland boat train from St Pancras. It seemed that in no time at all we had arrived at Carlisle but after that the journey across Ayrshire was rather long and tedious. Twice the guard announced over the public address system that the train would arrive at 18.29, so precise but to no one's surprise we came in ten minutes late. Where did the arrival time come from? Had it been inherited from the old days when clocks could be set by reliable transport? I sat next to a pleasant, mild man, once a missionary to Nigeria with the Irish Pentecostal Church, who was returning from some meetings in South Wales. I asked him the inevitable question about the church's attitude towards Ian Paisley but to his credit he wouldn't say a word against him.

The train arrived at the harbour, the majority of the passengers going to the Belfast ferry. I walked back to the town enquiring about buses, to be told that there were some during the day though not in the evening. I had to settle for a taxi. Then, having fixed a fare to Drunmore (the most southerly village in Scotland), I rather foolishly decided to go farther south, to Maryport. The cost of this additional mile (for which I was in no position to bargain) turned out to be, in pro-rata terms, out of all proportion to the original fare. Moral – decide on one's destination before negotiations start. Replying to my question about walking along the coast by footpath, the taxi-driver said, "Yes, that will be okay." To make doubly sure I asked someone else the same thing at the Maryport caravan site and received the same reply; the reality was rather different, with much scrambling over rocks, taking care not to slip-on seaweed, avoiding brambles on steep banks until I reached open fields at Mull Farm from where a road led to the toe of the peninsula, the Mull of Galloway.

At the lighthouse I asked a keeper for permission to camp on some flat grass inside the surrounding wall, but as he was reluctant to say "Yes" I retreated and found a quiet spot outside and pitched camp at the most southerly point in Scotland.

Saturday 18th May, to Portpatrick

Though I woke several times during the night, the lighthouse light didn't bother me as I had expected; in any case, night hours are short in Scotland at this time of the year. A local farmer had arrived by car at 6-o'clock looking for his sheep and I was up not long afterwards, breakfasting on London sandwiches. By eight I was on my way in fine weather, though a sea mist prevented me seeing the Isle of Man to the south, while a bank of cloud straddled the land to the north. First I went over the downs to Kennedy's Cairn, eight feet in height, substantially built with stones protruding to form a circular staircase on the outside. Some wag had left a glass bottle in the small hole on top.

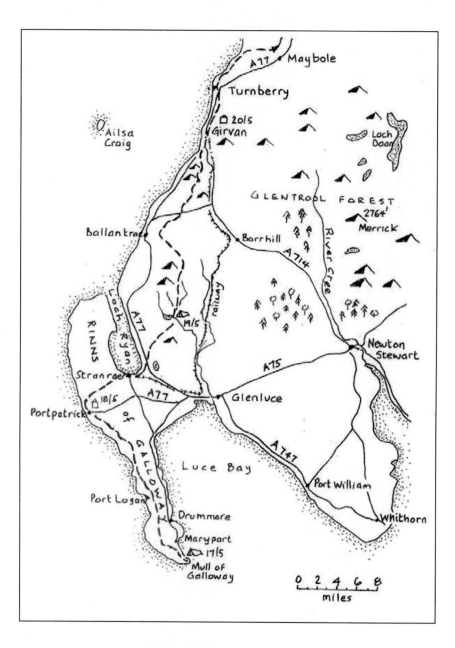

Mull of Galloway to Turnberry

After yesterday's difficulties I decided that cliff top walking would be too strenuous, so I retraced the road to Mull Farm, to an unnamed hamlet at the head of Auchie Glen and then by tracks to East, Mid and West Muntloch. At Inshanks an old lady had an Irish-Scots accent which was so broad that at first I had difficulty in understanding her. At Clanyard a pleasant young farmer spoke about this year's milk quotas: "If 1984 had been a profitable year, the 1985 quotas were not too bad, but for anyone who had had a poor year, they could spell ruin." However all the farms that I saw along the Rhinns appeared prosperous and new barns were being erected, some of which were the largest I have ever seen. My overall impression of this remote part of Britain was of a gigantic dairy farm, cattle and yet more cattle. When I mentioned that nowadays many people were becoming vegetarians, the farmer said, "Don't make me feel depressed." He asked me where I had come from that day. He then tried to impress on his fresh-faced, bright-eyed, six year old son how far it was to the Mull. The young lad responded with pride, "I've walked to Drunmore." (two miles) – good for you little fellow!

A pub lunch at Port Logan, a pleasant seaside village built on the south side of the bay. Here the quay was being rebuilt, though the landlady was at a loss to know why, as there were no published plans to dredge the shallows alongside. To the north of the bay is a tidal fish pond (rebuilt 30 years ago having been damaged by a mine in WWII), where the sea fish are so tame they respond to a bell, to be fed by hand. Though open to the public it is closed on Saturdays; so, no visit. Above the pond were the Logan Botanic Gardens, with lovely woods carpeted with wild flowers. Another five miles of tracks and footpaths brought me to Float Bay and then onto a road leading to Portpatrick, mostly walked in a haar sea fog, the same wall of cloud I had seen in the distance earlier in the day. Before entering this fog, I had been conscious of being surrounded by the sea, as the peninsula which forms the evocative district of the Rhinns of Galloway is only two miles or so wide. Outside the town the camping site charge was £3.00 for a night. As I had made up my mind that if this was more than £2 I would look for B&B accommodation, so I continued along the disused railway track, now a popular local walk, and found Mr and

Mrs Atkinson, a welcoming couple with a spick and span home. On asking for a sandwich for my supper I was given a full-blown meal.

After this refreshing feast I went to look around the town. In the harbour there were some fine looking yachts from Belfast taking part in a weekend race sponsored by the Royal Ulster Yacht Club. The crews were young and healthy, and possibly wealthy too judging by looks alone. They seemed a far cry from the Troubles.

Portpatrick is about 20 miles from Donaghadee and being the shortest sea crossing to Ireland it was an important place until Stranraer was developed to safeguard the larger steam vessels of the 19th century. The present harbour was designed by John Rennie in the 1820s, and to build it, a large amount of rock was removed in which, it was said, were the footprints of St Patrick.[15] The town is named after the saint because he is said to have 'strode' over to Ireland from here.

Sunday 19th May, to Stranraer and the moors
After an excellent breakfast, I left my comfortable accommodation at 9-o'clock and attended morning communion service at the Brethren Hall. There were two Brothers and seven Sisters at the service, the former making all prayers which were rather on the long side, reviewing most of the Old Testament as well as a little of the New, or

---

[15] Near the Mull of Kintyre there are footprints of St Columba's; also a chapel and well, reminders that this was where he landed in Scotland in AD563,

so it seemed. I was not permitted to take part in the service and rather regretted not going to the Parish Church where the service started later and where there was to be a presentation to the Sunday school superintendant who was retiring after many years of service.

My route to Stranraer followed the Southern Upland Way (a long distance footpath, a National Trail which starts (or finishes) at Portpatrick. The cliffs were covered with sea pinks and vernal squill, a purple flower like a small orchid, standing up proudly in the long grass. According to our pocket book of wild flowers this is a rare plant, occurring only in rocky pastures near the West Coast from Flint to Devon and also from Ayr and Berwick to Shetland. The genus Scilla, in which the bluebell was formerly included, derives from the Creek skyllo, to annoy, an allusion to the bulbs of the flower being poisonous. The flowers themselves were pure delight.

The way to Blackhead was varied and strenuous, first on top of the cliffs, then down to sea level by shingled bays and then across grassy downs. In Portamaggie Bay, below the Killantrigan Lighthouse, was the wreck of a steamer, the Craigantlet. She went aground on 26th February 1982 and still lay there in two pieces, largely covered at high tide. Above the bay a large tractor had been set up to salvage the remains of the vessel, large sections of which adorned the ground above the bay. A seal swam close by, no doubt making its own investigations.

While walking up the track from the lighthouse, I fell in with Tony Cooper from Birmingham. He had driven a furniture van to his friend Peter who was now living in the farmhouse at Moorcroft, rented for £8 a week. Showing more friendliness than the Brethren, he invited me in for a coffee. Pete had been unemployed and he and his wife decided to leave Birmingham and came here to live both a simpler and cheaper life. Both had found jobs with the local District Council and Pete designed the leaflets to help visitors find their feet on local walks. Though an excellent artist, as a student he had had differences with the staff of the art college and he left, "Because he didn't like to be told to draw this modern stuff". His forte was motor bikes and racing cars; he showed me some of his pictures including one of Mike Hailwood winning a TT race. Tony, his lorry-driving friend, runs a vintage motor cycle spare parts business which has been successful enough for him to open a branch in Holland.

After this welcome coffee break, I continued over the moors to Knockquhassen and then to Stranraer through a housing estate. Last Friday, on the suburban train to Victoria, I had bumped into a friend who, on finding that I was coming here asked me whether I would try and find a friend of his, to whom he had written but hadn't received a reply. On seeing a manse, I called and enquired about this Patrick Smith. The minister's wife said: "Yes, he lives in Bowling Green Lane which is off the main road, just beyond the railway line." It turned out that this was on my route and I easily found the house but Mr Smith was out. So, leaving a message with his son, I went on my way. Twenty minutes later, by the shore of Loch Ryan, a car drove up and the driver approach me. "Hello, Patrick Smith I presume!" We had a long chat and I passed on greetings from our mutual friend and he promised to write to him with the needed contribution for a Slavic Mission, before leaving him to continue on my way north. Having encountered the man in this way I rather expected a more exciting outcome, as had so often happened on previous walks but – *the wind bloweth where it listeth.*

Following an abortive visit to a deserted caravan site near Innermessan, trying to phone Iris without success and finding no café or shop to buy needed food – nothing since breakfast except the coffee – I took the moorland road to Ballantrae. According to Moir in his book *Scottish Hill Tracks*, this was the original road and on Green's map of Scotland (1679); it is shown ending at Innermessan which was an important place before Stranraer was built but which now does not even warrant a mention in the comprehensive Shell Guide to Scotland. The first part of the road leading to Penwhirn Reservoir had been metalled, a benefit to vehicles going to the modern filter station, but a disappointment for followers of old drove roads. Four miles farther on were some ponds, used each year as a nesting site by hundreds of black-headed gulls. When I was some way from them a sentry gull came and hovered above my head until I had moved out of their territory. The sight of all these gulls was impressive, the noise of their harsh cries deafening.

A car by one of the cottages near the filter station displayed Boy Scout stickers, encouraging me to ask whether I could buy some bread. The scout leader (who helped with a Group in Stranraer) kindly gave me some, refusing to take any payment, saying that if at any time he was in the same need, he hoped that someone would do the same for him. He also recommended using his tap water as the stream nearby was contaminated by effluent from the purification plant. So, armed with these essentials of life – bread and water – I went and found a pleasant spot beside the stream, pitched my tent but resisted a bathe in the effluent.

Monday 20ᵗʰ May, to Girvan

The morning dawned bright, cool and breezy after overnight rain. The metalled road continued for another five miles until Lagafater Lodge where there is a remarkable oasis of woodland in an otherwise bleak moorland. On the western side a screen of shrubs, mostly of rhododendrons, formed a gently rising shield, shaped by the wind and sheltering the taller trees and the more exotic plants, as well as the house. Walking through was moving into a different world, a veritable Garden of Eden.

In the real world of the moor the road became a grassy track which climbed to the 1500ft pass of Beneraid, on the way to which I met old Adam himself, exiled from the garden to cut turf. 'God', he told me, was now living in London but came to his paradise for holidays with friends. This Adam had been working here for more than 40 years and the spade that he had used over this long period had worn down to a quarter of its original size. He pointed out the landmarks on the distant horizon and told me about the tall solitary wall, seen on yesterday's road, which had been used for bombing and machine gun practice during WWII. Also of a 'factory' which had been built there for the same purpose.

Having enjoyed chatting with this weather-beaten man I continued over the pass and then dropped down from the high moor, leaving the ancient road two miles short of Ballantrae. The countryside was now mostly green and pleasant, full of prosperous farms, quiet valleys and wooded slopes. I bathed in a stream and then followed a zig-zag route to Colmonel where I had a tea and sandwiches in the local pub. The manager had no conversation, reading a book while at the same time watching a mid-day TV movie. The name of the town originates from St Colman as does the parish church, but here too I could find little of interest.

The map indicated a footpath on my planned route over the hill; as there was no signpost I asked a farmer working close by for confirmation of the path. He said there wasn't one. Taking the map as correct I continued up the steep hillside, finding some evidence of an old path but with obstructing walls and wire fences; the same applied to another footpath leading to Knockdaw Farm and a deserted farm at Barchlewan. Again, what should have been a good through walking route to Girvan proved very sketchy, with bog over the ankles at one point from which I had to beat an undignified retreat. At last I reached the pass under Cairn Hill and a view of the sea opened up. Ailsa Craig (popularly known as Paddy's Milestone dominated the scene, as it had throughout the day, but for some reason it rather depressed me. (Years ago, on a crystal-clear summer's evening Robin Coventry and I had seen this prominent seamark from the top of Ben Lomond, a distance of about 70 miles.)[16]

Having left my rucksack under a dry-stone wall, I climbed to the top of Byne Hill. On the train I had been impressed by these shapely Girvan hills, when they had seemed considerably higher than their 700 to 970ft. Free of my pack, I enjoyed running down the hillside before going on again, down to the sea, and then along the front to Girvan where I stayed for the night with a local and respected schoolmaster and his wife.

Tuesday, 21ˢᵗ May, to Ayr

The morning was bright but hazy and Ailsa Craig seemed less dominant today, perhaps because the light was different. Mrs Curry told me that last year a woman geologist had spent six months there by herself, studying the rocks and the only thing she had worried about was the rats.

Girvan harbour was picturesque and judged by the number of fishing boats and general activity. The two largest buildings in the town centre had been taken over by Building Societies, an all too familiar story.

---

[16] See End Notes.

not inclined to take the chance. In any case it was a lovely day, why should one complain when distant views over prosperous countryside were compensation enough for a hard road:

My feet are burnt; in blisters scalded
From walking these long roads of the King.
Peig Sayers

Before Ayr came Alloway and the Burns Country, with many up-market houses; how the poet would have smiled at all the prosperity he had brought to the area. The cottage itself was closed by the time I arrived and there was no apparent way into the gardens either. The roadside windows and door have been permanently sealed off from the dust and dirt of passing traffic, as well as from peeping visitors. So I did my own thing, climbed over a car park fence into a field and, by squeezing under the privacy hedge, snapped my camera at the celebrated house.

From here it was down to the seafront, along with evening joggers, cyclists and dog walkers enjoying the warm evening sunshine. The youth hostel, with its high surrounding wall and locked gates, was almost as difficult to get into as Burn's Cottage. I chose the long way round – there were no signs – before finding the entrance into a large baronial style house.

There were six or seven of us staying the night. The warden himself was rather 'upper class'. One of his activities was the leading of school journey parties, made up of groups of children from small schools in Stirlingshire. Next week he was to lead a party of 80 special needs children from Stirling; I wondered, were they from the same group I had met at Loch Morlich in1981.[18]

Wednesday 22nd May, to Arran
I was up at seven, breakfasted, packed and away before anyone else had stirred. The road into town was shared with commuters and children, hurrying off to work and to school. I was impressed by the substantial stone buildings; according to the local guide, Ayr has been a seaside resort since before the term was invented, with wealthy Glasgow merchants coming for short visits, liking the place and finally building their homes here. Out of the town I followed the coast by way of the golf course to Prestwick, said to be the oldest burgh in Scotland, but compared to its neighbour, a disappointment architecturally; best was the 15th century market cross. Next, the main road by the airport, with no sign of any international flights which arrive early and leave late in the day. As an airport it has the great advantage of remaining free of fog. Some say that it was a white elephant and there had been talk of closing it down, though an old man I met said that last year a profit of £2m had been made.

Two more golf courses brought me to Troon, a pleasant town with a lively Old Parish Church, judged by its informative magazine. There was more pleasant walking by the sea, with yet more golf courses, to Beach Park on the outskirts of Irvine. Here stands a huge leisure centre in which many activities could be enjoyed, for a nominal entrance fee of 10p (if I remember correctly). The town centre itself had been gutted and replaced by an extensive self-contained shopping centre, totally enclosed and with no obvious windows. I wanted some food but couldn't face going inside this monstrosity. The only other place in sight was a church, embraced by the shopping complex, which announced:

---

[18] See *Another Shore*, p178.

> CHURCH CENTRE
> CAFE SERVICE
> CLOSED BETWEEN
> 12.00 and 2.00

As it was 1-o'clock I decided to press on. The primary school teachers were on strike, the secondary teachers were not supervising school meals; consequently the whole town was running wild with children. O for a Pied Piper of Irvine!

An inland detour was required to get round the river Garnock estuary, with roads towards Kilwinning. On the way I met a pleasant lad, with his sister and friends, exercising some horses. He was a laboratory technician employed by a local firm; the horses, stabled on a nearby farm were a hobby. The young man was interested to know what I was doing since he had been on Outward Bound courses on Skye and in the Cairngorms. Earlier I had seen a party of half-a-dozen men, on their knees, weeding a turnip field, a sight reminiscent of the 19th century. The lad reassured me that things were not really as primitive as this but that the men had learning difficulties and were attending a course at a local residential farm training centre.

The ferry to Arran left at 6:15pm; she was the MV Arran, built as recently as 1984 and modelled after jaws, her huge mouth opening up to swallow cars and lorries whole. The crossing was as smooth as could be, and the ubiquitous gulls followed in her wake, glancing from left to right for tit bits that might be thrown away, though this looked unlikely as a notice warned:

> ANYONE THROWING THINGS INTO THE
> WATER
> IS LIABLE TO A FINE OF £100

I stayed the night in a Brodick guesthouse where the guests had to look after themselves as Mrs Smith, the owner, was involved in the island's production of Ruddigore in the village hall. (An old double-decker bus served as a dressing room and the final touches were being made to the production by a professional producer from the mainland.)

To the north here were grand views of Goat Fell. Many years ago I had travelled here overnight from London via Glasgow for a week's climbing holiday, found accommodation and was on top of the mountain by 4-o'clock, 18 hours after leaving home.

Thursday 23ʳᵈ May, to Lochranza

Contrary to the forecast of rain, the morning started as bright and sunny as could be. I collected a parcel of maps from the post office and sent home the discarded ones.

The first part of the old footpath into Glen Rosa was now a Land-Rover track; I met two fellows from Yorkshire about to start on a rock climb, by which time the clouds had spread in from the west bringing with them the promised rain. This glen is renowned for its wetness, draining in its short length a whole group of mountains but today, apart from a few boggy patches, it was relatively dry.

I climbed to the pass at the head of the glen and traversed along the western flank of Cir Mhor to find a sheltered spot for a bite to eat, then followed the connecting ridge up the other side to Caisteal Abhail (2815ft), missing the summit by 100 yards because of the enveloping mist and through not reading the map closely enough. This is the second highest mountain on Arran and one of the few hills I hadn't climbed on my previous trip and now I had failed by so little! My route continued along and down the northwest ridge to Creag Dhubh and then into Gleann Easan Biorach which was very boggy in places. On the way I met up with two pensioners, dressed overall in the latest heavy-weather gear, no doubt obeying the detailed instructions of a mountain safety leaflet before venturing into the hills. Rock pools invited a bathe to which I responded – but not for long, it was too cold. A cuckoo called and there were deer on the skyline but otherwise little else stirred. The glen ended with a flourish, the path threading its way through a small gorge and Lochranza suddenly burst into view.

Some food was purchased at the village shop – in a state of chaos as it was being rebuilt while goods were still being sold. The rain now set in for earnest; there was little to do except wait for the hostel to open. A crowd of friendly and lively teenage girls from Greenock Academy were there; they had recently finished their Higher exams and had come away on a Duke of Edinburgh expedition. Most of them were going on to University after leaving school. I joined three of them in a game of Scrabble but had to show them how to play to get points – they had no idea of playing to win! A young man from Glasgow had come here for some peace and quiet but made himself known to everyone; I cannot remember meeting anyone with a more amiable disposition. Later a school journey party from Hull arrived, bringing with them all the food needed for more than 50 hungry teenagers. Parties from this school had been coming here for some years, finding that it suited their needs admirably, for training young people in mountain activities. It didn't take long for the youngsters of this advance party to find friends among the girls and for a few hours there was a great deal of laughter in the corridors.

Friday 24th May, to Tarbert and beyond
Confusion with the timetable meant missing the first ferry of the day. A teacher, hitch-hiking from the Lake District, had also missed the boat. He was off to Jura to take part in a fell race over the Paps of Jura, popular because of the terrain but also because of the ceilidh which followed the race. Mike was lean and fit, living on trail-mix for his journey, so we persuaded the local café to open up and provide us with a pot of tea which, in the end, had to be downed in a hurry when the ferry arrived.

The ferry took eight cars and a great deal of expert manoeuvring was required to accommodate them. Finally we set sail, arriving half-an-hour later at Claonaig where there was nothing except the jetty and a kiosk. A pall of cloud covered the hills of Arran and mist covered the hills of Kintyre; then the sun broke through making the day more cheerful. The road to Skipness was quiet, far away from the busyness of Ayrshire and the grandeur of Arran. A number of caravans were parked along the water's edge, holidaymakers opting for a quiet time. At the village shop I bought some chocolate and a gamekeeper offered me a lift (in the wrong direction) and in talking to him he was able to direct me to a track leading into the hills. The only alternative route to Tarbert would have been a long way round by road. Before setting out on this track I made a short detour to Skipness Castle (13th century) which used to mark the southern boundary of the Campbell territories. The impressive ruins are now cared for by the Secretary of State for Scotland, a person with a lot of responsibility it would seem!

The way into the hills turned out to be a forestry road, unmarked on the map, taking me as far as a ruined croft at Glenskible. The misty clouds were down again to about 1000ft, and the terrain was not at all what I had expected from the map. Every bump seemed to be the summit I was aiming for, Cruach Doire Leithe (1240ft), the highest hill on the Skipness Estate. In the end the mist cleared and I found that I had missed the hilltop – the game keeper had said that it was difficult ground. I was now able to move more confidently to Mealdarroch Point where new forestry plantations were being developed. Here the ground was worse than a ploughed field but at last I came to another forestry road, possibly replacing the footpath shown on the map. Good I thought, but when this had taken me beyond Tarbert and beginning to climb back into the hills it proved a mixed blessing as I now had to drop down a steep heather-covered slope into the back gardens of Tarbert. It had taken me four tiring hours to cross the seven miles of hillside.

Tarbert harbour was filling up with yachts for a big race the following day and the shops were swarming with sailors, so after a bite to eat I left the town by the A83. A mile of road brought me to a path which led through three miles of parkland with many fine trees and extensive views over Loch Fyne. Halfway through the estate was Stonefield Hotel, built in 1837 with the well-known and greatest commandments inscribed on either side of the entrance doorway.

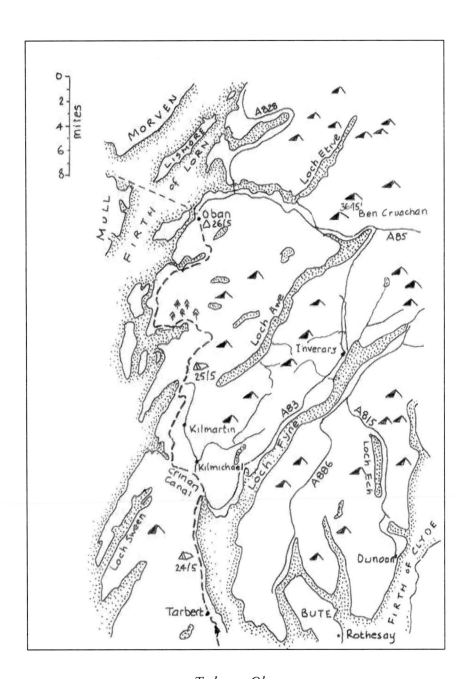

Tarbert to Oban

Thou shalt love the LORD thy GOD with all thy heart	Thou shalt love thy neighbour as thyself

Another four miles of the A83 brought me to Strachullin Farm where I camped, pitching my tent in the lee of a wooded slope, foregoing the scenic views across the Loch with a more exposed position; this was just as well in the breezy conditions. Nonetheless it was an altogether delightful spot, green grass, woods, a burbling stream, with cattle grazing on the hills – and potato cakes from Tarbert for supper.

Saturday, 25th May, to Kilmartin

After a good night's sleep, a bright morning dawned and I was able to make an early start. First there was four more miles of the A83 along the edge of Loch Fyne to Ardishaig where the Crinan Canal begins. The canal was designed by the great John Rennie in the late 18th Century, to assist the fishing industry by avoiding the sea passage around the Mull of Kintyre. There are a total of 15 locks for a total rise of 64 feet, along nine miles of canal. A party of three boats was beginning the voyage through the canal, with a fourth leading to make sure that the boats had a safe passage. It was relatively slow work for them as I was well ahead of this group by the time I had reached Bellanoch, seven miles along the towpath. At Cairnbaan there was an old fashioned grocers, almost unchanged from Victorian times, so old in fact that the food I was looking for wasn't to be had.

The small ferry shown on the map at Crinan no longer runs, so I had to leave the towpath at Bellanoch taking the road across the Moine Mhor (the big peat bog). Across the estuary from here is Duntrune Castle, also 13th century, possibly the oldest inhabited castle in Scotland. Then by track through Poltalloch where the estate house was a ruin, though the Episcopal Church was well maintained but little used.

In prehistoric times the area around Kilmartin must have been an important place. My brother Owen's friend, Leslie Grinsell[19] wrote to me saying that it was indeed one of the most spectacular prehistoric areas to be found anywhere in Scotland. There are stone circles, cairns and burial chambers, all well cared for. The inside of one of these cairns was lit by a glass roof panel enabling the visitor to appreciate the construction; I climbed down into it through a sliding trap door.

On leaving these prehistoric sights,[20] I followed a farm track to Carnasserie Castle, once the home of John Carswell. This man was the first Protestant Bishop of the Isles and in 1567 he published the Gaelic translation of Knox's liturgy, the first book to be printed in the ancient language of the Celts. A forest path brought me to the old farm at Ormaic, another path provided a route to the head of Loch Craignish, the only difficulty encountered being a six foot wall with no gate or stile. The scenery hereabouts was grand, with unexpected glimpses of the sea and with rock strewn hills looking far higher than their 700ft.

---

[19] Leslie Grinsell (1907 - 1995) was a self-taught archaeologist, specialising in the field identification of burial mounds (barrows). He was curator of Devizes and then of Bristol Archaeology departments and the author of many books on the barrows of Southern England.

[20] There is now a community museum at Kilmartin, dedicated to the ancient landscape of the area.

After taking another lane beside the Barbreek River, I came to Barnlaunich Farm where I asked permission to camp. The farmer found this an unusual request: it seemed that he had never been asked before. The tent was pitched in the rain and by 6.30 the wind was blowing strongly – it felt as though buckets of water were being thrown at my little home. Too tired to write my diary, I just lay down, relaxing in the snug warmth of my sleeping bag.

Sunday 26th May, to Oban
The rain had stopped by the time I got up at 7-o'clock, though the ground by my tent had become a small lake from water overflowing from the river which had risen by at least a foot. My first reaction was that I would have to back-track to the road. The thought of retreating was not attractive, so after finding a stout stick and wearing boots without socks in the prescribed manner, I braved the swollen stream and got myself safely across. A half-mile farther on the farmer at Turnalt told me of a new bridge near his farm – a better way to have crossed the cross swollen river. He also told me of a peculiar stone, shaped like a deer, further up the valley, which attracts a number of visitors but in spite of his instructions, I was unable to locate it. However, the walk through Gleann Donlhain was impressive, though I added a bit to the route through poor map reading, ending up on the road at Lagalochan. From here a scenic road by Loch an Lagalinnmor brought me to Melford where the post office was open and I was able to buy some essential food. Another track brought me to Melford where there were holiday cottages and classy boats at the private quay in Fearn Bay. The road to Kilchoan alongside Loch Melford was hilly, passing through lovely woodlands, the weather bright and bracing, changing to squally rain showers. A moorland track to Ardmaddy Castle and Auchnascaul took me back to metalled roads, and a signpost to Oban – still eleven miles to go. I had taken the zig-zag route around the peninsula to avoid the main road but this minor road, leading to the Isle of Sell and Telford's Atlantic Bridge over the Clachan Sound, proved just as crowded, it being bank holiday weekend. At this point I decided to feel unwell; remember correctly); many). I struggled on, hoping to find accommodation. There was none. Some miles farther on I saw a lady working at the bottom of

a large garden belonging to a hotel – Mrs Craig it turned out, was the manageress and, though off-duty for the afternoon, she welcomed me in with a warm-hearted smile, providing me with a mountain of wholesome sandwiches, tea and cakes, all for just £1.50. The hotel was advertised as 3-star, but sitting in a comfortable lounge in a leather chair, in front of a roaring fire, it seemed to me more like the Ritz. When I suggested that I might like to stay the night, I was told, "I'm very sorry, we're full up."

The final six miles to Oban proved to be much easier after this rest, especially as the rain had stopped. Coming into the town was rather tedious with ribbon development lasting for more than a mile. The expected view of the sea came only when I reached the harbour. All the shops were open, doing a roaring trade: it would seem that Sabbath observance on the West Coast is now part of history. The hostel, at the far end of the town, added another half-mile to the end of a tiring day. It was crowded with a school group and many others and I was lucky to find a bed in an annex. The wardens were a friendly Welsh couple; I'm always surprised to meet Welsh people in Scotland.

May 27th May, to Salen
Spring Bank Holiday and Scottish mist everywhere. I was still feeling rather out of sorts and in spite of getting up early I was the last to leave the hostel, going into town with a stocky, smiling Japanese fellow. He was on a nine month holiday in Europe and could only speak about two words of English; last night he had been writing copious notes in a diary which included all his public transport tickets with which to remember his travels.

As the Mull ferry didn't leave until mid-day I pampered myself with tea and toasted tea cakes. This was followed by a climb to McCaig's Tower, classified as a folly but Oban's most famous landmark and one which gives the town considerable dignity when viewed from the sea. Then, to escape the rain, I had more tea and cakes, this time in the Seaman's Mission.

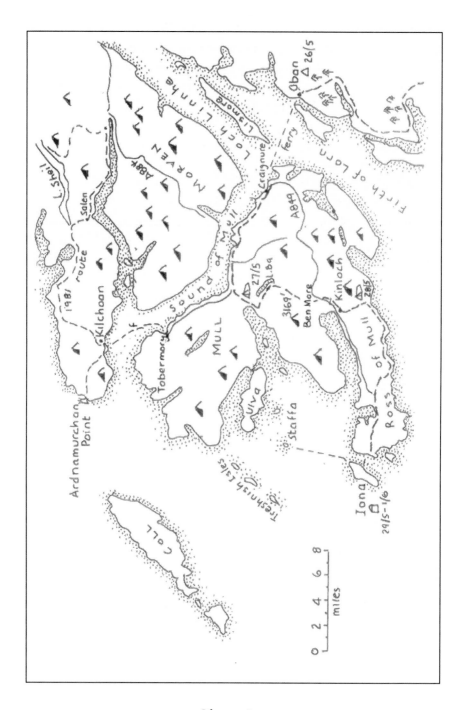

Oban to Iona

The ferry trip to Craignure was uneventful and, apart from continuing bowel troubles, there followed an equally uneventful twelve miles of road walking to Salen, along the Sound of Mull. What with the rain and upset stomach I was feeling rather sorry for myself and made up my mind to stay in the village for the night. But, after enquiring about B&Bs without success, I met a teacher with a group of boys from Prestatyn. They were camping three miles down the road, and as the weather had taken a turn for the better, I decided to walk on and join them.

Theirs was a delightful site (shared by a number of caravans) at Killchronan, overlooking Loch na Keal, at the estuary of the River Ba. This river originates from the inland loch of the same name and being only two miles long, it must be the shortest river in the Kingdom (as well as having the shortest name). The schoolboys were on a mountaineering trip. They were very friendly, only too pleased to help erect my tent, to collect stones to hold it down, to light my stove, to test my gear and to eat my food. They played football, threw spears, lit fires and ducked their mates in the icy water of the stream. Boys still seemed to be boys; for which, let us praise the Lord.

Tuesday 28th May, Ben More
I was awake at 6.30 on a bright, cold morning. Only two caravan women were up and about, hanging out some washing, and I had eaten my breakfast, struck camp and hit the road before any of the boys had stirred – I kidded myself that they would be most impressed with my early start.

Taking the track alongside Loch Ba, I encountered the first, and only, footpath sign of the whole trip (why are signs so scarce in this part of the country?), directing the walker not only in miles but also in feet to be climbed and suggesting hours for crossing the hills. The walk into Glen Clochalg was superb, with wooded slopes, a sparkling stream and mountains standing clear against the blue sky. Leaving my pack at the pass of Creag Mhic Fhlonnlaidh (1090ft), wearing shorts and taking only my waterproofs, I set off for Ben More (3171ft). The weather seemed to be so fine at this stage that I thought there would be no problems but another 1000ft up on the side of A'Choich (a subsidiary summit of the Ben) it became so cold that I considered retreating. However, after I had donned my waterproof jacket and leggings, I heard a dog bark and looking up spotted two people on the ridge ahead, giving me the spur to continue. There followed a strenuous climb on the ridge and 1 heard people talking by the summit cairn. Peeping over the low wall of rocks, I said:

"Thanks for the moral support you gave me; I wouldn't have got here if I hadn't seen you on the ridge. Where's the dog?"

"We haven't got a dog."

"Which way did you come up then?"

"Oh, we came up from the road, down there."

"Didn't you see two people? One of them had a yellow anorak; they had a dog with them. I heard it bark."

"No. No-one came up your way."

"Are you quite sure? I saw them coming up the ridge."

Whatever became of that other party was a mystery – one of the strangest experiences I can recall in all my wanderings.

The other summit party comprised a mother from the Lakes, her daughter and son-in-law. They kindly gave me a drink of tea from their flask, short on flavour but very welcome. The clouds were bowling over the summit, bringing with them flurries of snow (my earlier body temperature hadn't lied) so I said, "Thanks a lot, I'd better be off," and beat a hasty retreat, back down the ridge, running a loose scree slope, then onto larger blocks of scree until I was on the grass and met up with my pack. Thence down to a road leading to Kinloch Lodge Post Office where I met my friends from Ben More; they had come on by car and couldn't believe I'd got down so quickly, though I was equally surprised to see them, now looking relaxed and much warmer than on the summit of Ben More.

I continued along the road to Carsaig, an oasis of green fields in a sheltered bay by the sea. Then, following the high ground for a short way along the coast, I camped among the grass and heather overlooking the sea towards Jura and the Garvellach – the Isles of the Sea – glinting like jewels in the evening sunshine. Legend has it that it was on one of these islands that St Brendan the Navigator built a monastery, where St Columba went to meditate away from the noise of Iona and where these two met when Brendan was about 90 years old. Altogether as exhilarating and as pleasant a day as one could have wished for.

And in his cell beside the sea,
The Celtic saint has prayed for me.
John Betjeman

Wednesday 29th May, to Iona
Again there were rain showers during the night, the morning covering the hills to the north and east. It was easy walking on grassy downs above the animal tracks which wound their way between lakes and across valleys which cut their way down to the sea. The cliff scenery was dramatic; in some ways it was like a mountain ridge with rock towers and with the ground falling away on the landward side as well as down to the sea. There were wild flowers and birds to gladden the heart, a skylark rose from under my feet, giving its nest away. A party of wild-looking, unshorn sheep ran ahead of me, sometimes peering down at me from the heights, sentry-like; when I also stopped and looked back, one of the cliffs rose high in the air like a gigantic fang. At another point, possibly Binnar Ghome, I stopped, waiting for the clouds to clear as the sunshine slowly crept along the coast from the west, so that I could get a better photograph. These were perhaps the most dramatic cliffs I'd ever seen but the map gave little idea of what to expect.

Things changed a bit at Traigh Cadh' an Easa, a deep valley cutting down to the sea on the far side of which there was a new forestry plantation, protected by a high wire fence hugging the cliff side. My first reaction was that I would have to return from whence I'd come, my second, to give it a go. Fortunately there was just enough space between the fence and cliff to get by, with an animal track for encouragement. Occasionally hanging onto the fence for support, I finally scrambled down at Cnoena. There was a herd of wild goats at the old hamlet of Shaiba; I was told later that they had been left behind when the hamlet was evacuated in the 1920s. From here another track, not shown on the map, brought me to Scoor where the old farm had been converted into a holiday home.

My impression of the area was of little agricultural prosperity. There appeared to be few cattle or sheep on the farms, much of the land has been given over to forestry and within a decade or two the landscape would have changed considerably. W.H. Murray in his book *The Islands of Western Scotland* wrote that: 'Mull has good land and that scores of acres could be reclaimed for farming and crofting at a third of the cost of tree-planting.'

My original intention was to have continued along this southern coast line to Iona, but route finding was now proving difficult, even in the fine weather; it was also tiring work through the heather and bracken. When studying the map at home it had seemed so easy; now I had a much greater admiration for John Merrill, who came this way on one of his long journeys and seemed to have taken everything in his stride (as it were). So from Scoor I took the farm track leading to Bunessan and from there on the road to Fionnaport and the ferry to the island of pilgrimage.

Iona didn't let me down: it was everything I had anticipated and more. The light was dazzling. The sea was so clean that the coloured sands and seaweeds showed clearly through the sparkling water. And then the historic buildings and standing stones and crosses – the sights were such that my camera was always on the go. But best of all perhaps was the peace and tranquillity: with virtually no road traffic, it was so quiet.

Ideally I would have liked to have stayed at the Abbey where there was a programme of activities for church and other groups, run by the resident staff of the Iona Community.[21] Individuals can usually join in but as all the spare places had been taken up I arranged to stay with Mr and Mrs MacDonald who had a house next to the quay. With a base established I was able to attend the early morning and late evening Abbey services and to make some explorations.

---

[21]   See End Notes.

Thursday, 30th May, Iona

After breakfast I had a long chat with Mr MacDonald. In 1926, after much hassle with the landowner, he had bought his present house, the old blacksmith's shop, the roof of which had originally been thatched. He was rebuilding it when his wife became ill and he had to stop. He then moved to Glasgow where sadly she died. After remarrying some years later, he was appointed the ferry-master on the island, a job he held with MacBraynes for eleven years during which time the four boats under his charge did not suffer a single mishap.

Then, in the 1950s, he was able to start rebuilding the old house which was a credit to his workmanship. He still dug up horseshoes from his garden which he cleaned and painted, pouring scorn on some others on the mainland (Mull) who sold 'their' shoes as 'Ionan'; nor was he much in favour of the Iona Community – he felt that it had spoilt much of the old ways on the island. Sadly Mr MacDonald was crippled with arthritis, though his mind was fully alert and he loved nothing more than a good chat.

With all the talk I didn't get away until one o'clock. I borrowed a map of the island from my host and made a tour of the southern part of the island. After going to West Bay, I climbed Druin an Aoinedh (the hill with its back to Ireland) so named because St Columba was unable to see his homeland from there, and confirming his decision to stay. Then I went on to Columba bay, which retains the name Port na Curaig (the bay of the osier-bark) in memory of the Saint's landing on the island, to bathe in the clear, cold water and to admire the variety of smooth multi-coloured pebbles. From here I tried to find the elusive granite quarry, but without success scrambling over numerous headlands, having many rests to savour all the sights and sounds, until I returned to the village for an evening meal, the Abbey service and bed.

Friday, 31ˢᵗ May, Staffa

A local tourist boat left at 9.45 for Staffa and Fingal's Cave. The weather remained fine and sunny and the crossing was calm and pleasant. The island and its caves were more exciting than I had ever imagined. I thought that if this place had been discovered in the South Seas everyone would have raved about it, yet here it was on our doorstep. As far as this journal is concerned I cannot do better than to include two paragraphs by Tom Weir:

> Ah, how I would like to have been Sir James Banks who sailed with Captain Cook in the Endeavour and who was the first tourist to land here in 1772. He came with tent and food for two days, having been told that, ". . . no one even in the Highlands had been there." Banks came to look at the pillars, described to him as being like those of the Giant's Causeway. Scrambling up to the crown of the island he found a bothy, and in it a herdsman leading a solitary life, looking after cattle grazing on the green crown of the island. It is the next bit I especially like. The herdsman insisted on Banks and his companion sharing his hut. He

set down fish and milk before then regaled them all evening with Gaelic songs.

They spent the night scratching themselves and by morning they discovered they were lousy, and Banks mentioned the matter, expecting some sort of apology to his reproach. At which the herdsman bridled, telling them with some asperity that they must have carried the vermin with them since there were none before they came.

The ruin of a bothy is the only sign of habitation today. Stone steps for the convenience of tourists lead up the cliff, concrete had been laid, and iron railings fixed, in the MacBrayne era to safeguard tourists traversing from the jetty into the great cave which extends for over 200 feet into semi-darkness.

I was more impressed than I had expected by the scale and the rock architecture exposed by the pounding of the sea. Describing it, Banks asked the rhetorical question: "Compared to this, what are the cathedrals or the palaces built by man?" Banks was told it was called the cave of Fhinn, Fhinn MacCool (hence Fingal's Cave). Long before it was known to the Gaels as Uamh Binne, the cave where the sea makes music and no doubt it was the sounds of the sea in the rocky cave which inspired Mendelssohn to compose the Hebridean Overture after his visit in 1829.

Along with others I spent an hour or so watching the antics of several hundred puffins on the far side of the island. These charming birds would sit by their nesting sites, quite happy for us to be there, knowing that if we came too close, all they had to do was to fly off to the sea. Then our time on this magical island was over all too soon.

Before catching the last ferry of the day to Iona, I spent the rest of the afternoon walking the coastline, from Fionnphort to Knockvologan, close to the island of Erraid (which once maintained a heliograph serving the local lighthouses). Nearby, on one of the small islands, was a colony of seals, sharp silhouettes in the clear water,

Saturday 1ˢᵗ June, return to London

I was up at 6-o'clock, determined to make the most of my stay. The whole island seemed to be asleep, as I made my way to the north end of the island to climb Dun Auchabhaich, at 310ft Iona's highest point. From this summit one could appreciate many of the inner Hebredian islands, standing out from the sea as on the rim of a gigantic wheel, with the observer at the hub.

A last Abbey service, a last meal with the MacDonalds before I caught the first ferry of the day, to join many others on the coach to Craignure. While waiting for the Oban ferry, I had a happy reunion with the boys from Prestatyn and the summit party from Ben More, all of whom had enjoyed their holidays. Oban now basked in sunshine and holidaymakers thronged the streets; there was a long wait here for the train to Glasgow, and then the overnight train to London.

Apart from the usual crop of happy memories, I also brought back a splendid suntan. I was asked more than once: "And where have you been for your holidays?"

- 3 -

The Outer Hebrides

Friday, 16th May, to Oban

The journey to Glasgow was as pleasant at it could be, on a sunny day the clear sky was strung with white cotton wool clouds and England stretched out on either side like a beautiful garden, wide open for all to see. I sat opposite a retired surgeon and his Scottish wife, going north to visit an elderly aunt. For many years he had been closely involved in the research for the cure to TB. When his wife got on the train at Euston she found that someone had parked a bag on her reserved seat; she asked in an imperious voice:

"Has this seat been TAKEN?"

"Yes," I replied.

"It CAN'T be. It's been BOOKED," she said indignantly.

"Well, taken by mistake then."

Anyway, she got her seat back, happily bore me no grudges and we continued in conversation for the rest of the journey.

In Glasgow I was able to visit a college student, to advise him on his referred design project. Back in the city centre the shops were rapidly closing – including my favourite cake shop – and there was just time to buy provisions for my journey. Close by a lonely preacher had taken possession of the library steps in George Square, a young Church of Scotland minister in training shoes, his bicycle used as a billboard for displaying his evangelistic posters.

There was a longish wait for the Oban train of ancient rolling stock. The journey seemed to go on forever and I felt less than enthusiastic about mountain scenery which displayed considerable amounts of snow, especially on the north facing slopes of Ben Lui. The Oban youth hostel was crowded with the children of a French school party; and, among others, two youngsters on a cycling trip (following the completion of their O-levels) and the driver of a van supporting a team in the Three Islands Race. This annual event involves each team sailing a yacht from Oban to Troon and on the way climbing Ben More, the Paps of Jura and Goat Fell, all in the weekend. Later, two mini-vans arrived with members of the Edinburgh University Highland Society who were off to Mull and Iona the next day; they described themselves as: "Less energetic than the University ramblers, who were in turn less energetic than the mountaineers."

Saturday 17th May, to Barra

A leisurely day, waiting for the afternoon ferry. In the post office I wrote first-day covers for next Tuesday, which the Postmaster promised to stamp and send. In a side street the Oban Pipe Band was warming up, before marching through the town to the local park for a band competition. As always, it made a stirring sound, adding colour to the day and, as a pied-piper, attracting a crowd of children many of whom were dragging their parents along as well. An athletics meeting was taking place at the same time; a pleasant afternoon was in prospect but when it started to drizzle, the proceedings were somewhat dampened. The bands, each roughly 20 strong, included girls and women; many of the bands had come long distances by coach to take part.

There were about 50 passengers on the ferry to Barra, some going on to Lochboisdale where the boat was to stay overnight. The weather was exceedingly grey, so that much of the excitement of the voyage through the Sound of Mull was lost. However, through the gloom we were able to see Tobermory and the Ardnamurchan lighthouse, the most westerly point on the mainland and then three hours to cross the Sea of the Hebrides to Castlebay. By now the sun had come out, lighting up the guarding island of Muldoanich, which, in a wild sea, looked like a set for a Wagnerian opera. Castlebay was rather disappointing, the houses scattered; Kisimul Castle,[22] the only significant medieval castle in the Western Isles, seemed much smaller than I had expected.

All B&B accommodation was full except one; this proved friendly though rather scruffy – but with wind and rain lashing down I was glad to have a roof over my head. There were six children in the family, the three eldest away at school in Stornoway. Eight-year old Jim, the next in age, button-holed me to play chess.

Sunday 18th May, to Eoligarry
Before breakfast I took a stroll, around Castlebay. There were some fine new buildings under construction; a school, a leisure centre which included a small swimming pool and, close to the sea, a new cottage hospital. (On my return to London I wrote to the architects and engineers responsible for these projects and they kindly supplied some plans which were used for project work for my students.)

Jim persuaded me to play some more chess and it was ten o'clock before I got away, along the west coast road of the island. Two miles on at Halaman Bay, a distinctive new hotel caught my eye. From a distance I took it to be a factory building and wondered what comment Prince Charles might have to make about its architecture. Later I learned that The Highlands and Islands Development Board had paid £5m for its construction. The original hotel operators couldn't make it pay and so they had sold it to the owner of two of the island's other hotels for £46,000. Part was converted to self-contained holiday flats and the new owner received a grant from the HIDB to finance the conversion. He was then about to return this back to full hotel status and he might have got a grant for that too.

---

[22] Kisimul Castle is the seat of the Clan MacNeil. The first of the MacNeil family to have settled in Scotland was Hugh Aonrachan, King of Airleach and Prince of Argyll, descended from the Irish King Niall of the Nine Hostages in AD397.

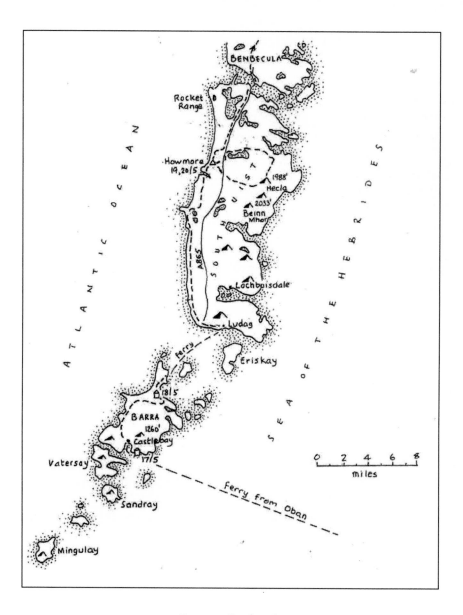

Barra to Benbecula

Several of yesterday's ferry companions were on the road, some on cycles, some walking and one couple with three young children, who had started out by car from Mold in North Wales. They were looking for a camp site and planned to spend several days on the island before continuing their holiday on other islands. I thought about that family several times during the week, wondering how they had coped with the gale force winds.

Five miles farther on is the Parish Church at Cuier, the only Protestant one on Barra, and I arrived just in time to attend morning service. The singing of hymns was taken at a traditionally slow Scottish pace, though possibly the organist was unable to raise the tempo. A sprightly octogenarian, the Rev Roderick Mackinnon, was leading the worship in English, with the concluding grace in Gaelic, the sound of his voice and the sound of the words brought a lump to my throat:

Gras ar Tighearna Iosa Criosd:
gradh Dhe, ar n-Athur:
comh-chomunn an Spioraid naoimh:
gub robh maille ribh uile. Amen.
The grace of our Lord Jesus Christ:
the love of God our Father:
the fellowship of the Holy Spirit:
be with you all. Amen.

By the time the service was over, the early fine weather had been replaced by wind and rain and in the lee of the church I put on my waterproofs. A wooded copse at Northbay provided a welcome sight to an otherwise treeless island and from there the road led to Eoligarry Ferry, passing the airport which uses the shell beach for its airstrip. The goose-neck lights for landing had only recently been installed; before that, night landings were completed with the aid of the light from suitably placed car headlamps.

At Eoligarry I enquired about overnight accommodation. There was none. So I wandered down to the jetty where, for the benefit of prospective passengers, there was a small hut, with a loo and water tap. There was also some level grass but unfortunately the site was so exposed to the south-westerly winds that there was no possibility of pitching my tent. As I took shelter in the cabin a car drew up encouraging me to enquire again about somewhere to stay. The driver informed me that the nearest was at the house belonging to the owners of the shell factory[23] beside the airport. Not relishing retracing my steps against the wind, I asked if he could give me a lift. "Yes," he kindly replied, although first he had to make some local visits and be back in an hour. As good as his word, he returned to take me to my night's lodging.

The driver told me something of himself. He and his wife had been running a caravan site in Argyllshire, but they had returned recently to the island where they had been born and brought up, so that their two children could also grow up here. He would now earn his living by fishing, having bought a half-share in a new boat some two weeks previously.

Mr Harold Couzens, a smiling, open-faced man of about 60, welcomed me as their first paying guest. It turned out that the bungalow had been built by Sir Compton Mackenzie. Externally the building was rather plain and, from the road, partly hidden by shell tippings; inside it seemed like a small palace, with a long central corridor and two wings of bedrooms in what used to be CM's billiard room. The windows of the house are permanently sealed to keep out the wind and rain. The old feu of the house required that if it were destroyed, by fire say, it would have to be rebuilt in exactly the same style. As the cost of rebuilding (at the then current prices) would have been something like £500,000, requiring an enormous insurance premium, the Couzens decided that it would be safer (and cheaper) to buy the feu. They had another home in the Lake District, and another mining business, and commuted by car between their homes for periods of up to a month. (London commuters, note well.)

The 'business' entailed extracting shell from the beach, and something like ten tons was needed to produce one ton of useful roughcast which was then mostly exported to the mainland. The waste material was returned to the shore, sometimes sandbagged to help with the drainage of the air-strip. The firm used to employ a manager and a dozen men but, as business had fallen off with the recession, they were (at that time) able to employ only two. They had had problems with

---

23 In 2014 the firm had changed to Crushed Barra Shell Ltd.

MacBraynes, the ferry company, who were apparently notorious for losing things. Some rope slings for hoisting the bags of shell (posted two weeks previously) hadn't yet arrived.

Over a five-star dinner the Couzens told me several stories about Compton Mackenzie who had built the house in 1936 for £5,000, which was raised by loans from his friends. When he came to the island there were no metalled roads and because of this, he refused to pay his motor tax. For this he was fined £100, later reduced to £5, but the final outcome of the various protests was the construction of the road around the island. He also helped to set up a Seaman's Trust to protect the rights of the local fishermen. On his death in Edinburgh his body was brought to the nearby local cemetery and the 50-year-old piper leading the procession died from a heart attack while playing the lament!

The Couzens also spoke of the fish processing plant that had been built recently, opened the previous year by Prince Charles. Local people were complaining about its effluent discharges, polluting the loch, ruining the fishing and creating an awful smell. But so far these complaints had failed to move the establishment – it's 'too political'; as Peter Walker had reminded the nation after Chernobyl, "We're a democracy. It can't happen here."

Monday 19th May, to South Uist and Howmore
The total cost of my overnight stay was £13.50 – the most I had, then, ever paid (except in Norway) but it was money well spent compared to a sleepless night in the jetty shelter. How I would have dragged out the hours there I don't know. Harold gave me a lift down to the ferry in his Renault 5, too small a car, one would have thought, for all the travelling they do, to and from the Lake District.

The 25-foot passenger ferry, arriving on schedule, was owned and operated by Donald, a youngish man. He had the largest pair of hands I have ever seen, though with the lightest of touches on the steering wheel. The wind had dropped and the sea crossing to Ludag was uneventful.

Clive James from Caernarfon, whom I had met on the ferry from Oban, was also on his way to stay at the Howmore hostel so we joined up for our walk. This was mostly by track along the machair of the western shore. Disappointingly there were few flowers – spring had yet to arrive to bring the abundance of wild flowers for which the machair is celebrated. We reached our destination in six hours, arriving at about 4-o'clock when we were fortunate to meet the travelling shop and buy some food.

The Howmore hostel is run by the Gatliff Trust,[24] a small charity which then owned three other similar buildings in the Outer Hebrides. These are in traditional stone-built cottages with thatched roof, two rooms, metal-framed bunk beds and gas cooking. So far just ten people had stayed this year but many who do stay make enthusiastic

---

[24] The Trust was set up in 1961 by Herbert Gatliff (1898 - 1977), a retired Civil Servant, to perpetuate his many charitable interests. These included, in particular, encouraging the enjoyment and care of the countryside of England, Wales and Scotland by the young especially through youth hostelling.

comments about the location and scenery. The warden, Mrs McQueen, a quiet and softly spoken woman about 75-years old, lives in a similar cottage close by. She had been looking after the hostel for 18 years.

During the evening the sky cleared revealing the mountain range on the eastern side of the island. We explored the small village, especially the old church ruins scheduled as an ancient monument. According to John Starkey it was once a mediaeval priory with an international reputation but destroyed after the Reformation in the 16ᵗʰ century. The ancient chiefs of Clan Ranald were buried here and in fact the name *howe* is derived from Old Norse, meaning mound, barrow or place of sacrifice.

We also looked over the modern Scottish Presbyterian church which was open, well cared for, comfortable and clean. The main chapel area included a long communion table down a centre aisle, giving the visitor an impression of a warm, friendly, Christian fellowship.

Tuesday 20ᵗʰ May, Hecla

Clive's itinerary was more ambitious than mine; while he went to climb Beinn Mhor, Ben Corsdale and Hecla, one of the classic routes in the Outer Hebrides, I went for Hecla and it took me just two hours to reach the summit though it looked, and felt like, a substantial mountain for all its being only 1998ft high. The view to the north when I came onto the summit ridge was splendid; the eastern, indented coast stretched away to Benbecula with sparkling lochs and lochans, green and brown hills jumbled and sunlit. The wind from the south-west was now bringing with it sharp, stinging rain showers. Loath to face them, I continued to a second lower summit before following ridges east and then north down the eastern flank to avoid the cliffs of Beinn na h-Aire. From here, looking at the dark, swirling clouds which had gathered behind me, the mountain seemed remote and forbidding. It was under a rock on these bleak slopes that Bonny Prince Charlie waited for Flora MacDonald, to bring him news about his planned escape to Skye.

My route brought me by Loch Spot, then a stream to Loch Skipport and a track to the B890 road. The map showed a path across the peat bog which lies in the middle of Loch Druidibag, which I was unable to find. Using my compass for the only time during the day, I failed to make contact with the central causeway but was fortunate to find another way across to reach the road-head to Drimsdale village. I have often crossed extensive farmland on a compass bearing, following the route of some ancient footpath lost to the plough, and most usually reached the desired point but here, with Howmore church on the horizon and with a bird watching-tower as landmarks, I failed to find the right way. However, this route-finding failure actually brought me closer to the Howmore shop and hostel, arriving at four o'clock.

Clive was already back, having completed his own tour. He related his adventures which included being followed by a local dog which had joined him at the shop. This animal accompanied him for the whole mountain circuit and, as with most energetic dogs, walked and ran twice as far as his human companion. Clive enjoyed the dog's company and had to share his only chocolate bar. A recent entry in the hostel log-book also recorded a dog joining two people across these same mountains; an animal of some character it would appear.

Wednesday 21st May, to North Uist and Baleshare

There was a loud knocking on the door at breakfast time and a man in his 30s came in, cold, wet and fatigued. He told us that he had failed to reach the hostel last evening having walked during the night and through the rain. Having got thoroughly wet he had sheltered for some hours in a telephone box; a more uncomfortable situation it would be hard to imagine. We gave him some hot tea and, as Clive and I were leaving, he went to bed to thaw out and catch up with his sleep.

We followed the machair toward the rocket range, but there was no shelter here and squally showers soon had me soaked to the skin. But then the weather cleared and the day remained for the most part fine and sunny with clouds dominating the sky, driven by westerly winds; it was a marvellous day for being in the open air, with outstanding sea-, sky- and landscapes.

After joining the main road, a minor detour was made to view the impressive statue of the Madonna and Christ Child, erected through the energies of the local priest in part protest against the presence of the rocket range close by. Army personnel were coming and going in their cars – I gave a friendly wave to one and received a regimental salute in return, as from a clockwork soldier. Then it was back to the main road and a café break, just before the causeway joining South Uist with Benbecula; after three hours of walking I was ready for a meal.

The causeway had been built seven years previously. Low tide revealed large expanses of sand across which one could have walked, and before the causeway this was indeed where travellers crossed between the two islands. A motorised digger was eating away at the sandbanks, loading lorries; one lorry had been filled with seaweed.

A memorial for Benbecula recorded the names of 50 soldiers who had been killed during the WWI but there were just two in WWII. The island tarns are black with peat and these contrasted strongly with the blue-greens of the sea. I left the road for Rueval 400ft high, the only hill of the island. The view from the summit is renowned for when the sun lights up the 365 tarns (it is alleged that there is more water than land in Benbecula); today the view was not all that impressive, even though the weather was clear. The walk down the north side of the hill to rejoin the road was enjoyable until I hit a maze of peat workings near the road.

Two miles of single-lane causeway joins Benbecula and North Uist; this one had been built during WWII. Once again there were good views of the distant hills of North Uist, the sky constantly changing as shower clouds came in from the west. The walk into Carinish was against cold, driving rain; there were no shops here as one might have expected, though an old man was delivering the morning newspaper at 4.30pm.

I reached Baleshare soon after five o'clock. Here, the Gatliff Trust hostel is a small thatched cottage, over 200 years old, with walls, some three foot thick.[25] Mrs Tosh, the warden, lived in a new bungalow close by. She told me that her great-grandmother came to the old house as a young married girl and that both her grandmother and her mother were born there. She enjoyed being close to the old house, with all its family associations, happy in the knowledge that it was well maintained and being put to good use.

---

[25] Baleshare hostel is no longer in the custody of the Gatliff Trust.

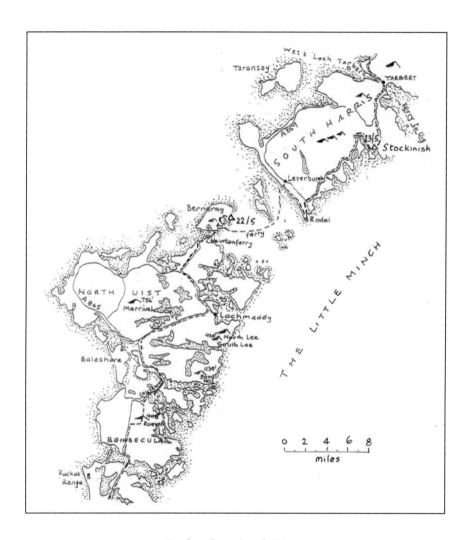

Benbecula to South Harris

As I crossed the field to reach the hostel a dozen hens followed me to the door, no doubt for scraps of food but I was one up on them having obtained some of their eggs from Mrs Tosh. Clive, who had made a general tour of Benbecula using buses, was already installed; there were lambs at the door when he came in – animals it seemed were attracted to him.

During the evening there were heavy showers, followed by a brilliant double rainbow. Later, in spite of those 3-foot walls, we could hear the wind howling outside.

Thursday 22nd May, to Berneray

We had a lazy breakfast but the poor weather dampened our enthusiasm for the day's journey across North Uist. Finally we plucked up courage and left at ten o'clock, with Clive and I going our separate ways (to meet up again later). Five minutes along the road, unable to find my watch I retraced my steps to the hostel and then found it strapped to my wrist!

A pleasant track across the moor brought me to Clachan where there was a shop and post office. From here it was to be a metalled road all the way to the north end of the island. The chambered cairn under Ben Langas, 200 yards off the road, deserved a visit. A notice at the entrance read:

> Chambered or tunnel cairn
> continuously used in the 3rd and
> 2nd millennium and also by the
> Beaker Folk (early Bronze Age)
> It is dangerous to interfere with
> the structure.

After 4000 years?

I crawled through the doorway on hands and knees, the chamber lit by light filtering through cracks between the large stones. No experience came to me except the hardness of the stones on my knees, unlike John Starkey who had a painful experience here (recorded in his book *The Road through the Isles*). To measure the radiation count inside, he took a Geiger meter into the chamber; while sitting on a ledge in the semi darkness beneath the long stones supporting the great mass of the mound and looking at the light filtering through the passage stones, the world gradually receded as the sound of the meter clicking filled the space. After 20 minutes he received a kick in the kidneys which sent him flying forward against the rocks. He said that he was lucky to escape minor injuries from the large, protruding stones, but the sudden nervous shock and a sore back for days afterwards were more than sufficient to repay him for his morbid curiosity.

Farther along the road I was overtaken by yet more squally showers, one so vicious with stinging hail that I had to seek shelter behind a pile of peat – there was no other refuge along this exposed road. Even so, and despite the bleakness, the trek across the island was enjoyable. Waves broke spray over the windward shore of the inland lochs and one fisherman, a 70-year-old, was doing his best to cope with his rod in the wind. A regiment of conifers had been planted on the hillside, perhaps to test whether trees can survive here. The peat hags were neatly cut; one lone man was out, far from town, cutting away but with no sign of transport.

Lochmaddy is the main port for North Uist; except for the harbour, there was little there – a bank, a post office, a few shops including the WEEHAVIT SHOP. Ugh. After having dinner in the hotel I made post-haste along the island's eastern road to be in time for the ferry to Berneray. The wind was difficult to cope with at first; occasionally a car would stop to offer me a lift. The uneven road had some short stretches upgraded to dual carriageway and, near the B893 junction, a quarry company used the road for access to its operations which straddled the road.

The green of the machair at Robach and Newton, with sheep and cattle grazing contentedly, was a welcome relief from the bleakness of the moors. A sign directed passengers to the old jetty, cars to the new. Following these instructions I arrived in time for the ferry, but this was going to Harris, not Berneray so I had to retrace my steps to the car ferry, the Harris boatman promising that he would phone to let them know that I was on my way.

The new jetty, built some five years ago, had been financed by the EEC. Before this there had been no car ferry to the small island of Berneray; soon there was to be an airstrip there as well. Clive was waiting, having arrived some two hours before me. Several lively, friendly school children were on board for the 15-minute trip.

It seemed a long walk along the edge of the bay, through the island's village. We were able to buy food at the open-all-hours-shop, before going on to the Gatliff hostel at Baile. The place was locked and as no one was around, we walked back towards the shop to be told that the warden lived at Besdarra, about a mile away to the north. Luckily, before going there we checked again at the hostel, to find the key hidden in a crack in the doorway.

This traditional island house, recently renovated by the Trust, was like a small palace, just ten feet from the seashore. A peat-fired Aga stove kept the place pleasantly warm. The roof had been rebuilt with timber trusses, overlaid with marine ply and straw thatch, a finish which gave the building a traditional look. The internal stone walls were painted white and there were several dean kitchen surfaces for food preparation. At the time there were only six beds with more planned in an extension – the chemical loo was still housed in a ramshackle hut. The warden paid her visit to make sure we were comfortable and later the young assistant ferryman delivered a bottle of gas. He was accompanied by an ancient who spoke with a pronounced Glaswegian ascent (he had spent many years living and working in Glasgow); he was only too pleased to come along to spy out the renovations.

The ferryman told us something of the local fishing on this relatively prosperous island. The boats are now 25 to 30 feet in length, considerably smaller than the older boats which were expensive to buy and maintain. The new boats were each operated by two men, weather conditions usually restricting fishing to four days in seven. At that time they were fishing for prawns; later in the season for lobsters which were taken to Holyhead for final preparation and sale. The fish are sold by the men of each boat, an average weekly catch earning them about £750. A fishermen's cooperative arranges for the purchase and sale of materials such as fuel and rope.

Prince Charles went to stay on the island for three days that spring, to help a crofter set his potatoes. Apparently the tabloid press had created a fuss because he had gone there for some peace and quiet but who could blame him for wanting to stay on such a beautiful island.

Friday, 23rd May, to Stockinish

Clive was still asleep when I left the hostel. We had said cheerio last night as he was going to have a lie-in before spending the last day of his holiday exploring Berneray. He had been good company over the last few days, keen to speak and learn Gaelic; he had brought a mini-library with him and his pack seemed to weigh a ton.

I arrived at the pier in time for the 9.15 passenger ferry but need not have hurried as it was 15 minutes late. On board were four local people and three cyclists from Stoke. The latter had come to Lochmaddy last night after a rough crossing from Oban, waves breaking over the boat, the journey time one hour longer than usual. Our crossing (in a much smaller boat) was relatively smooth, in bright, cool, breezy weather and full of interest. Across the Sound of Harris, the ferry used a route to the west of the scattered islands to avoid the wind-swept eastern shores. Hundreds of gannets were fishing, diving into the sea at great speed and from every conceivable angle. Seals came close to the boat. The water sparkled with spray and dancing waves – no wonder there was a campaign to keep large oil tankers from using the sea lanes between the islands and the mainland. Our landing was at Leverburgh, named after the margarine king who had attempted to bring more prosperity to Harris and Lewis. The town was to have been a major fishing port but after some major building work and one very profitable season's fishing, Lord Leverhulme died. His successors then closed the place down, selling most of the assets, and now all that remains is the harbour, the road to Finsbay and a few houses.

I followed the road along the south-west coast of Harris, passing the villages of Carmanish and Strond, and then a mile of delightful footpath winding through the hills close by the sea, to arrive at the remote village of Rodel. Here, St Clements Church, well known for its monuments, is used today only for occasions such as weddings. The fabric was maintained by the Department of the Environment;

scaffolding around the tower had been erected the previous year and masons had recently started work on repairs to the roof and the coping of the tower.

The Rodel hotel was also undergoing repairs but was somewhat lacking in service. I had a bowl of soup and a sandwich for my lunch, rather different no doubt from the time of a royal visit in 1956 – a plaque on an outside wall commemorated Queen Elizabeth landing here in that year. Her signature, together with those of Prince Philip and Princess Margaret, are framed in the church.

Four hours and 13 miles of twisting, turning road cutting its way through a rocky, peat bog landscape, enlivened by views of the sea along the south-east coast, brought me to Stockinish youth hostel. The young, recently installed, warden told me that the previous post-holder had stayed for just three hours. The building had been the village school, there was no food to buy here and backpackers' hopes rested with a mobile shop which occasionally passed the door.

The Stoke cyclists were there: Ron, close to my own age, Philip and Tony. The two 20-year-olds were arguing with their older companion about returning to the mainland as quickly as possible – they could see no virtue in being there at all. We played chess and followed this with a card game which was new to me, over which we had many laughs. Among others who were staying, there were three OAPs, all carrying heavy packs, and an Australian nurse who had been on the road for about a year, travelling as she felt the need and in no particular hurry to move on.

Saturday 24th May, Tarbert and a mountain pass

I was away from the hostel at 9-o'clock, following the road to Tarbert via Crier, the cyclists passed me enjoying a fast ride in a following wind. A lamb was trapped on a ledge, bleating and unable to reach his mother and farther on I was able to warn the crofter of the animal's plight. Near the town an older woman was out for a stroll and we chatted as we walked into town. She was a farmer from near Sherwood Forest and had been to Scotland for a clan meeting – by all accounts this had been so hectic that she had come for a few days to wind down before returning home. She thought that there was a lot of waste on

Harris, instancing bags of fertilizer lying unused on the ground: "Who paid for these?" she wondered.

Rhenigidale is a village six miles to the east of Tarbert and I had hoped to stay there, at the Gatliff hostel. This little place is one of the remotest in the islands and at that time it was only possible to reach it by walking or by taking a small boat. Thus, Mark Douglas Home, writing in the Independent in 1987:

> Three days a week, Steven McCombe sets out from Rhenigidale, a wind-swept crofting community to collect the mail. He leaves at 7.30 a.m. walking the rough, sometime steep path from the village to the Tarbert road about 4.5 miles; it takes him two and a half hours to reach Tarbert. Then, with letters, newspapers, and shopping for the 11 villagers, he returns home, a round trip of about 12.5 miles. The path is the only overland route to the village of eight houses, a school, a youth hostel, and a telephone box on the exposed coast beside Loch Seaforth. The nearest road stops abruptly 2.5 miles short of the community. But now, in the final years of the twentieth century, Rhenigidale is at last to enter the age of the motor car. In 1989, a single-track, tarred road will connect it with the rest of Harris and Lewis. And the villagers, who have longed for such news for years, are delighted. Kenny MacKay, 52, who has lived there with few interruptions all his life, said: "It will make a world of difference."

Without the road, the village might have died. In the last century, 100 people lived there, supported by crofting and fishing. At the time of my trip, three of the houses were empty and there were just two children at school. When Mr MacKay was a child there were fifteen.

Mr MacKay, who had just started a salmon farming business, believes that the road would bring economic and other benefits. He foresaw a growth in sheep rearing, the village's staple industry, and in tourism. The villagers already owned three cars – but they were parked a very long walk from home.

Sadly, I learned that the warden of this Gatliff hostel had died recently, that the building was in disrepair with a leaky roof and that it had been taken over by a tramp. The staff at the Information Centre were unable to help me with other accommodation in the area.

After a meal at the Quayside hotel, I went to see the ferry leave harbour and met up again with Ron, Philip and Tony who had finally agreed to return to the mainland. I waved them a goodbye, stepped back to take a photograph and just avoided falling into the sea – through an unguarded hole in the planking of the temporary jetty. Having regained my composure from the thought of a fatal accident, I made haste to the McBraynes ticket office to make a complaint to the manager. He was quite abrupt with me and considered that no one should have been there anyway. I pointed out that even if there had been adequate warning notices any child could have walked onto the temporary decking and fallen through. He was not impressed with my arguments. So on leaving town, I passed the police station and decided to register a formal complaint; after all, a stitch-in-time might save a life. The constable was friendly:

"Who was it?" he asked me.

"The MacBraynes' manager," I replied.

"Yes, he is like that, but despite appearances he has a kind heart. I will see what can be done."

On returning to Tarbert a few days later, I went to look at the hole and found that a guard rail had been erected – the constable had obviously been as good as his word; praise the Lord for small mercies! After my journey, and back in Bromley, an entry in the church magazine caught my attention. Michael and Jackie Cranefield had written in their newsletter from Zaire:

> The new school term .... has just begun. On the first day of term the students have to pay their fees and there are always problems. Only half of the students turned up; the others were delayed by family problems, lack of money or transport holdups. One of Michael's students arrived but without his school fees – he had used up all his money trying to get his father out of prison. His father had been jailed because he had been digging a hole for a toilet and had left it unguarded while he took a break for lunch. A

child fell into the pit and was killed, and the unfortunate man was held responsible and thrown into jail. Many other reasons prevent students from arriving on time for the school term, but within a week everyone is usually settled back in.

I sent a copy of this to the policeman, with suggestion that he show it to the manager and thank him for having erected the safety rail.

The day's previously mild and sunny weather gave way to rain as I took the road to Meavaig. I was able to shelter from the worst of this in a shed, joining company with a lamb who had the same idea. Later, at Ardhasaig, I spoke to a kindly, rather old-fashioned lady selling Harris tweed and knitted garments. Her son ran their croft. During our conversation I asked her about Finlay M...., an author and broadcaster, one of whose books I had recently enjoyed reading. She became angry and close to tears at the mention of this man, ... his lies..., his book. He had left his wife and 15-year-old daughter for a young singer, who had in turn left her young child. She recalled that he had been a brilliant schoolboy but having heard one of his radio talks ("full of lies") she certainly wouldn't read his books. She was glad that his parents were not alive to know about it.

I left my rucksack in a roadside hut at Meavig to go on for a mile or so to phone home. The public telephone was out of order but the family of the house, against which the phone booth stood, welcomed me into their kitchen and with Highland hospitality fed me with homemade scones, cake and cups of tea. A daughter, the nurse responsible for the old people's home in Tarbert, was visiting her mother, while her father and husband were out cutting peat. Two grandchildren came in from play, well mannered, rosy checked. The public call-box was their telephone, but at present they could only receive incoming calls! So they suggested another cottage along the road and from there I finally made my call to Iris, who was in good spirits.

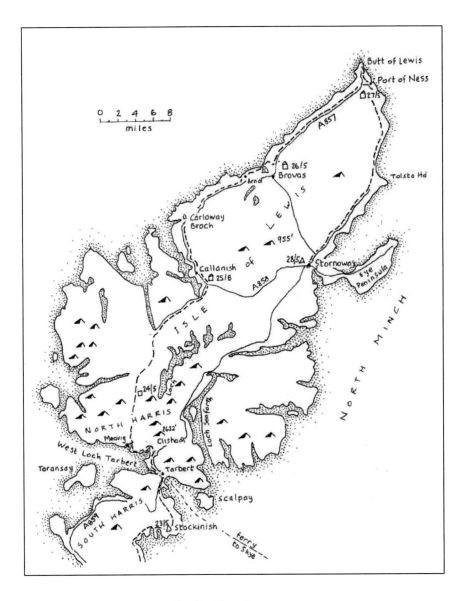

Stockinish to Stornoway

I rejoined my pack to make my way through a pass between two ranges of steep, craggy mountains. Five miles of well-made track gave way to ankle and knee-deep, boggy ground. My hope had been to reach the head of Loch Resort (the boundary between Harris and Lewis) where there might have been shelter for my tent, but then I came across a little bothy, with two wooden bunks, one with an air mattress, and here I decided to stay. This was well-timed as by now the wind was increasing to gale force, rain was lashing the corrugated sides of the little hut, with a single perspex sheet roof light and the door jammed shut with a timber beam. As there were still several miles of boggy track and streams to negotiate before reaching the road by Loch Roag – the ground I had already crossed had been bad enough – I would have had to consider backtracking if the weather didn't improve. The Selkirk bannock[26] (this long-lasting, nourishing loaf should be recommended to all long-distance walkers) bought in Tarbert would last me two days – there seemed little chance of walking in that weather.

It was a wild, wild night; the wind screamed, rain and hail lashed the hut. My hopes of a comfortable night were dashed when the air mattress slowly subsided under my weight and occasional drips of water onto my head told me that this temporary home wasn't as watertight as I had imagined. Rain driven under the door created a puddle on the concrete floor which had to be mopped up.

Breakfast – one cup of tea and a slice of Selkirk bannock. Waiting for the weather to improve, I was undecided about what to do, but by 10.30 the conditions had become considerably brighter and I decided to press on. The ground was boggy, slippery with surface water and my feet went from under me .... slow down .... take it easy .... these were the orders for the day. However, the rivers were fordable and the remaining showers gave way to a bright and sunny day. Keeping away from the deepest bog, suddenly life was good again.

---

[26] The Selkirk Bannock is made from wheat flour and large quantities of raisons. Robbie Douglas was the first known baker who opened a shop in Selkirk in 1859. When Queen Victoria visited Sir Walter Scott's granddaughter at Abbotsford she is said to have had her tea with a slice of Selkirk Bannock thus ensuring its reputation for ever.

At one time the track which led northwards to Morsgail Lodge would have been a well-built and well-maintained path; here and there was the evidence of little stone bridges but now most had been reclaimed by the bog. Some of the worst stretches had been covered with old car and truck tyres which might be good for vehicles but didn't do much for the walker. The sheiling at map reference 131000 consisted of two beehive huts, one almost intact, a small doorway for men and beasts. The bridge at map reference 133212 was down, the river too fierce to ford, but a path on the south side of Loch Morsgail with a bridge at its north end, saw me through to the estate road. The eight map miles had taken me just over three hours, not too bad considering the terrain, far better than night-time fears had imagined.

The road to Springcorrie was being straightened out, new cuttings being blasted through the solid rock, making redundant all the delightful bends which had followed the contours of the land. The road work was funded partly by the EEC, partly by the Army who had played havoc with the old road by using lorries to transport sand which had been excavated from the machair. For me it was a quiet, pleasant day; no work was taking place on the Lord's Day, otherwise it might have been a dusty, noisy walk.

At Callanish I booked in at a B&B close to two stone circles, the more celebrated stones standing on the skyline, half-a-mile away. Four other guests were staying for the night. One Australian had led an active, interesting life including time in Spitzbergen and Greenland on oil company business. A keen sailor, he had skippered a Bristol Cutter for a brother who owned holiday yachts and this year he and his wife had booked on what may be considered as the ultimate in package tours – a 7-day trip to Easter Island.

Monday 26th May, to Barvas

After a leisurely breakfast, talking with other guests about Easter Island and other exotic places, I went for my own tour of ancient stone monuments. The Callanish megaliths are amongst the most remarkable in Britain but they were not what I had expected from the pictures I had seen in books. Nonetheless, they were most impressive. The stones, recently cleaned of their lichen by the Department of the Environment (though not to everyone's liking), resembled a group of modern sculptures. Erected four millennia ago, they had been dug out of the peat into which they had sunk over the centuries. The main avenue is 300 yards long, the whole group set out in the form of a cross with three lines of stones radiating from the centre, south, east and west. Disappointingly they were enclosed by wire fences. There were tea rooms close by, otherwise it was very non-touristy.

After Callanish my route north followed the A858 about a mile from the coast; walking the shoreline is almost impossible as the crofts, separated by wire fences, run in narrow strips towards the sea. On almost every croft were the ruins of blackhouses with a new bungalow close by. Occasionally a blackhouse was used as a garage or shed but most were occupied by sheep or birds. The scenery, still rocky and peaty, was becoming less hilly.

Thence to the Carloway broch, built on a small knoll sloping steeply towards the south and west. This 2000-year-old defensive castle-cum-home is the second best preserved in Scotland. The visitor can go inside the keep and walk some way up the staircase within the double skin walls.

After the visit to the broch, I passed a croft and, heard the sound of chattering machinery; a rain shower gave me an excuse to see some weaving. A young lad was working at the loom, an apparatus which had been made in 1940, but which hadn't been used for the last ten years until the youngster had taken it over. My first impression of this young man was not optimistic but first appearances proved deceptive. He was quietly spoken and helpful. He told me that he had started work on a fishing boat but one weekend, having caught nothing and being cold and wet, decided that fishing was not for him; so he left this work and took up weaving, the trade of his stepfather. It had taken him three months to learn the skills: he pedalled away as we talked, changed over the shuttles and all the time there was a rackety noise.

"Could he sleep when he first started?" I asked him.

"No problem," he replied.

"Why don't you wear ear-muffs?" I asked in my ignorance.

"Because I wouldn't be able to hear if anything went wrong – like the breaking of a thread."

In all that noise? I marvelled to myself.

A new loom cost £10,000 but he preferred the old ones, which were more reliable, he said. In fact he had just bought another second-hand machine for £500. He was able to produce on average two, 38-yard lengths of cloth a week, each sold for £65. This took him about four days but he didn't necessarily keep to regular hours, sometimes he started at nine in the morning and would go on till ten at night. Some weavers like to work each morning from six to nine, and then go out to their crofts.

The rolls of cloth are left by the roadside, to be collected by van for the distributors. During the day I saw three firms collecting bundles and in the townships, mostly from huts or sheds or garages, I could hear the never ending chatter of the weaving machines.

Swifter that a weaver's shuttle,
my days have passed and vanished.

....

Remember that my days are like a breath.
Job 7: 6, 7

At Shawbost the children's museum is housed in an old church building. Several people had mentioned it to me, praising this venture which had started in 1971 in response to a Highland Schools project. It is now on the tourist trail. Many interesting exhibits had been collected and arranged over the years by the children. Some relatively long-term archaeology was being undertaken, including the restoration of an old grinding mill. My impression was of a need for more care in the presentation of the collections – perhaps this was completed after the renovation of the building, which had been promised by the local council.

Recently erected new bus shelters were made of pebble-dashed, prefabricated reinforced concrete, designed to serve as windbreaks from whichever way the wind blew. They seemed out of character with the surroundings; more imagination by the local council could have provided attractive shelters made from local stone (of which there was more than enough lying around) and at the same time providing employment for two or three masons and apprenticed youngsters.

A mile or so further on at Bragar another attraction, a pair of 20-foot whale bones forming an arch, with a harpoon slung between them. They had been erected between two gate posts, probably part of an old house but unrelated to the present buildings. No plaque, no notice, no explanation.

At Arnol I left the main road to visit the tourist blackhouse, a pair of buildings, the living room and the barn, which had been bought and renovated by the Scottish National Trust. A mother and daughter, the original owners, were the custodians who lived in a modern house built close by. A peat fire was alight in the middle of the floor, the smoke percolating through the thatch – a worthwhile visit for understanding the recent past, but worlds away from suburban England. The last blackhouse in these islands had been vacated as a dwelling about ten years previously, this one around 1960.

From here I took a track across country. Unable to locate the footbridge shown on the map, a wire sheep fence straddling the stream had to be negotiated to reach the far bank. This grassy verge would have made a good camping place, but the blackhouse warden had already kindly telephoned a Mrs MacDonald for accommodation at Barvas. Also a phone call home was due.

On leaving Brue I worked my way along the coast, enjoying the feel of machair under my feet, and the sight of the sea breaking onto cliffs, sending spray high into the air. Care had to be exercised when I came to the nesting ground of hundreds of terns, birds of great individual beauty – but creating in me a feeling of near panic from their shrieking cries.

B&B at Barvas where Brian from Ballantyre, a young insurance manager, was staying for a week as he worked with, and encouraged, the firm's local agents; and a London couple from Wimbledon who were touring the islands.

Tuesday 27th May, the Butt of Lewis
My watch had stopped during the night and the smell of frying bacon made me jump out of bed. The early morning was calm and bright but this soon deteriorated into the forecast strong winds and driving rain requiring me to shelter in a garage. Then it was a foot slog along miles of relatively straight, featureless road in damp dismal weather. A number of cars stopped, offering lifts, the Travelling Bank kept pace with me to Ness; all the villages looked similar, built hugger-mugger, the few houses with any style were most often those built from local stone.

At Cross primary school, a few boys were out playing football. Bright, clean, rosy-cheeked, handsome children; they came to chat with me, anything for a diversion. I asked about their holidays and one little fellow said:

"I wish I didn't have to go to school at all."

"Where are the rest of your school friends?" I asked.

"They won't come out because of the weather."

Brian had recommended a certain Mrs McDougal of Lionel for my night's accommodation. Having reached this village thoroughly wet and tired, I was disheartened to find her out; however, as is often the way, I was administered island hospitality by one of her neighbours. Mr Gunn was a salt-of-the-earth man, 25 years a skipper of his own fishing boats out of Stornoway; pictures of his two vessels hung on the wall. He had had to sell up because of rheumatism. A large barn was built onto the side of his house and there he maintained, among other things, a clinker-built boat from the Orkneys, used for occasional local fishing out of Port Ness, in company with his son.

By the time I had dried out in the Gunn's warm kitchen, the weather had improved and a walk to the Butt of Lewis was called for. Without my pack I covered the couple of miles in no time at all and enjoyed a visit to one of the remotest spots in the UK; a shaped wooden plank on a cliff edge had the simple inscription:

> A. Martin
> 4/5/53

No other warning was necessary to keep away from the sheer cliffs.

A German family arrived, in a great hurry to take photos of everything in sight, before moving on to the Callanish and the 9-o'clock Stornoway ferry. I thought that it was only American tourists who had no time to pause for breath and enjoy the scenery. I suggested that they should also visit the Calloway broch as well and hoped that they did, but probably it was too much also to hope that they would miss the ferry!

On my way back through Five Penny Ness I went to visit the tiny St Olaf's chapel, named after a saintly Norseman. This well-maintained building had been erected in the 12th century, though the site was ancient enough, having been consecrated in the 6th century by St Moulag, a contemporary of St Columba. There was a Celtic preaching cross in the small churchyard. In the 10th century it had become an important place of pilgrimage for people suffering with sores, and regular public worship had continued without interruption until recently. David Livingstone's Prayer Book was gifted to the church, though this is now kept at St Peter's in Stornoway.

Ness and the other villages of the area boasted a sports centre and a football club which won the North of Scotland Cup some years ago. This was a creditable achievement as there were only four teams on the island and they played mainland teams in the cup competition. There was some street lighting; trenches were being dug along the roadsides to place electricity cables underground, to minimise damage from gales. But why not bury the telephone cables at the same time? No doubt BT would dig its own channel, such is the haphazard way we do things in Britain.

Wednesday 28th May, to Stornoway

> *Stornoway is great, with its castle,*
> *the largest town in the world except Dublin in Ireland:*
> *surprising it is that the king himself does not reside therein.*
> an old island saying

Breakfast at 8-o'clock for an early start, but in the end I didn't set out for *the largest town in the world* until 10.45. First there was a visit to the grocer's shop for a film – still shut at 9.45. Then a visit to Port of Ness to see the small boat-building yard (also shut) ran by Mrs MacCleod's brother-in-law – the area has some tradition of boat building. Return to the grocer's to buy the film; back to Mrs MacCleod to collect my pack plus another coffee and chat; it was such a friendly, no-sense-of-urgency place that I felt like staying for a week. Then I took the road south.

The metalled road continues for two miles or so before becoming a track followed by peat bog. Mr Gunn had told me that much of the road-building on the island had been initiated by Lord Leverhulme and the plan had been to have a complete road encircling the island; in the end the final ten miles across the worst terrain along the north-east coast was never completed. He had a caravan at the end of the road and he related how one day, when he was there enjoying a quiet time with wife, a German motorist arrived expecting to drive on to Stornoway – his map showed a non-exsistent road.

From the Gunn's blue caravan I was able to follow the dip in the ground which was to have been that road. This track gradually petered out and from then on it was tough going over the peat hags. At Asashahadar there are summer sheilings, huts which were still in use; on the cliff close by are the ruins of an old Baptist chapel, last used for worship more than 100 years ago.

The weather was now improving and for the first time on the trip there was summery weather, enabling me to shed my anorak and walk in a T-shirt. On the high part of the moor were some great skuas, large birds and new to me. I was tempted to visit their nesting sites, built on rocky outcrops, but decided that caution was the better part of valour; just as well, a colleague at work told me later, as these birds will not hesitate in going after an intruder when their nests are approached. Beyond here the sea cliffs were reached, with grassy sheep tracks, and I was able to sit and bask in the warm sun. My reward was the sight of a school of pilot whales swimming northwards, close to the shore, rising and falling in the water in a leisurely fashion. Five boats were fishing on the Minch.

The fine weather didn't last for long; having resumed my way across the moor a rain squall descended in great fury and it became a fight to get into my waterproofs. All too soon, the fun of this lonely stretch of country was over and I reached the track which became the beginnings of a road at the *Bridge to Nowhere*.[27] At North Tolsta I met a couple from Hitchen (I had seen them at Rodel) and was invited into their Bedford van for a cup of tea and cake. They have taken the van all over Britain, and in the process had completed more than 300,000 miles – it was then on its third engine. By the time we had finished chatting it was nearly four o'clock.

The walk into Stornoway, a 15-mile road slog, was a bit like walking into a London suburb – there were trees, a marked contrast to the many days of bleak moorlands. And also, praise the Lord, far less litter here than in the other areas. The Outer Hebrides have often been described as one of the last unspoiled areas in the UK; the scenery is indeed beyond compare, but visitors also describe these islands as the last resting place of the motor car – old cars were left to rust away on nearly every croft. Caravans on crofts were often damaged by gales and then disintegrate to an unsightly pile of debris, beer cans and bottles discarded in the peat workings and on the roadside. On my return to London I wrote to the Scottish Tourist Association to suggest that their brochures might contravene the Trade Descriptions Act.

The last four miles was in company with a 27-year-old, a father of six children, going into town to help at the YMCA to which was attached the then only self-catering hostel in Stornoway. This was one of the few places where teenagers could meet their friends, let off a

---

27   The Bridge to Nowhere was the end of the road from Stornoway to Ness, planned by Lord Leverhulme, but never completed. According to Wikipedia the mixing of many tons of concrete was done by hand (!) with some 140 men employed with wages of up to 10p an hour – generous wages in those days.

bit of steam and play games such as snooker. When we arrived, these youngsters were busy playing on the noisy fruit machine.

By 11-o'clock the young people had gone and a blackbird was singing his delightful song on the roof outside my window.

Thursday 20th May, to Skye and Raasay

In the summer months dawn comes early in the far north; at three o'clock the blackbird was singing again, not such a welcome song, outside the window.

For breakfast I finished the Selkirk bannock that had been kept for emergency rations; it had come a long way from Tarbert. Though the morning was dull I enjoyed my tour of the town – the first large town since Oban, twelve days ago. The abundance of trees, dressed in spring green, continued to delight, the harbour busy with fishing boats and a variety of shops. An ironmongers, founded in 1864, seemingly unchanged since its early years, reminded me of Iris's and my discoveries of our own family history.[28] It was all so interesting that I nearly missed the bus to Tarbert.

The ferry to Uig was a clean, well-founded boat; a calm sea and friendly fellow passengers made for a pleasant journey across the Little Minch. It was the first time that I'd been to Skye but as soon as I arrived I wanted to leave – this popular island seemed overcrowded; so I caught a bus to Portree and Sconser for the ferry to Raasay; here was a pleasant contrast, a place of quietness, a variety of scenery and especially some magnificent woodlands. There was no store at the youth hostel, so a travelling companion and I bought food in the local grocer's shop; we had gone into the little post office where we tried to leave our packs but were refused permission, since: "There might be a bomb in them". One cannot be too careful in the outer isles.

For those with simple tastes the hostel was perfect: warm, comfortable and overlooking the Sound of Raasay towards Skye. The building, a memorial to Alan Evans, had been renovated in 1982 with grants from the Cross Trust and the HIDB The warden, Rona, an OAP, made us all feel welcome and concerned for our needs. This

---

[28] One of the 'family' shops owned by Brown & Colby was a similar ironmongers as late as 1980; see *The Colby Connection – a* family history.

lively lady had always been interested in young people and open air life. Finding time on her hands when she retired from teaching, she decided to offer her services to the YHA for the summer period – husband and daughter had to shift for themselves.

Friday 30th May, home

There had been much talk of three pairs of eagles during last night's natter so I decided to get up early to see them for myself, a 5-mile walk before breakfast. But waking at 4.30 on a bleak, grey morning proved to be not the best time for me – and I went back to bed; a wretched confession.

On my walk back to the ferry, Rona passed me in her car; she was off to Skye to get some petrol and other essentials. She kindly gave me a lift to Broadwater and on the way related a few stories about her intermittent life on Raasay. Once she had a party of artists and one of the young ladies was out painting on Sunday; an old man, waving his stick at her, shouted: "You heathen girl you – painting on the Sabbath!" There were two churches on the island but Rona was unable to accept the strictness of their way of celebrating their Christian Faith. In some ways she regretted this as, if she had been able to attend worship, it might have helped her acceptance by the local people with whom she had found it difficult to make friends.

Rona also told me of a certain Dr. G...., a Harley Street specialist, who had bought the island of Raasay in about 1970 but had never lived there. Whenever the islanders wanted permission to do anything he would always say "No", so that he became known to them as Dr No. One of their requests had been to build a pier and, as permission from the Doctor was never forthcoming, the Scottish Office eventually requisitioned enough land for the pier to be built. The mansion belonging to the estate was an historic building but as Dr No never lived there, it fell into disrepair; the roof began to leak and many valuable books in the library were ruined, as was much of the antique furniture. Skyemen used to remove bits and pieces from the house, openly taking them on the ferry to the 'mainland'. Eventually, after Dr No's death, the HIDB took over the house to be used as an outdoor centre, though a lot of money was required to bring the house back to good repair.[29]

Then it was bus to Kyleakin, five minutes on the ferry to Kyle of Lochalsh; thence by train to Inverness, Edinburgh and London, arriving home at 8-o'clock the following morning to find Iris still in bed, my travels over for another year.

<hr />

[29] Once the clan seat of the Macleods of Raasay, Raasay House has been completely refurbished. It is now run by a private company a private company offering holidays, outdoor activities, celebrations and special events.

END NOTES

Achiltibuie

On another walk down the NW coast I was able to visit Tanera Mòr where Dr Fraser Darling spent many years studying grey seals off the Coigach Peninsula. On the same trip I visited the hydroponic greenhouse at Achiltibuie and was most impressed by the project. I later found out that it was not commercially viable. Alison Graham (of the Achiltibuie Garden Ltd) wrote:

> *As you know, hydroponics has been used in Achiltibuie for many years and the old Hydroponicum which you visited was started by the then owner of the Summer Isles Hotel as a way to grow fresh produce for his guests. The Hydroponicum was then taken into private ownership and run as a visitor attraction for a number of years. When it was next offered for sale in 2006 (at which time it was not commercially viable), my colleagues and I took over the running of the business whilst the land and buildings were bought separately. After successfully completing the 2007 season we took the decision to move the business to a new site over which we had more control and built our current Keder greenhouse at the end of 2008. We have continued to use hydroponics because it is an ideal method for growing a high concentration of plants in a small space: we sell all our produce locally and still invite visitors to tour our growing space and learn about hydroponics. The original greenhouse was finally demolished last winter – very sad to see it go, but it had become derelict and was a danger to the public.*

Gruinard Island

Gruinard Island was the site of a biological warfare test (anthrax) by British military scientists during the Second World War. Then for many years it was judged too hazardous and expensive to decontaminate the island sufficiently to allow public access. In 1986 an effort was made to clean up the island and a flock of sheep was introduced, which remained healthy. In 1990, the island was declared safe and it was repurchased by the heirs of the first owner, for the original sale price of £500!

Knoydart

In 1948 an unsuccessful land raid was undertaken by the 'Seven Men of Knoydart' who attempted to claim land in the ownership of the estate for their own use. Their claims were contested by the estate owner, the Second Baron Brocket who took the case to the Court of Session which ruled against the land-raiders. An appeal to the Secretary of State for Scotland was rejected and the Seven Men gave up their fight to obtain crofts on Knoydart. A cairn commemorating the Land Raid was unveiled at Inverie in 1981. Issues were eventually resolved when the John Muir Trust helped establish the Knoydart Foundation, which purchased the 17,000-acre Knoydart Estate in 1999. This was an historic moment for Knoydart and one that the Trust had spent 16 years trying to bring about.

Ailsa Craig

Ailsa Craig is an island of over 200 acres, ten miles from the mainland, where blue hone granite is quarried to make curling stones; it also gives its name to the well-known potato and is famous for the granite from which curling stones are made. The island, colloquially known as Paddy's milestone was a haven for Catholics during the Scottish Reformation in the 16th century; today it is a bird sanctuary, a home for large numbers of gannets and puffins.

Robin Coventry was a neighbour from Kirkintilloch days, a wellknown Scottish artist who sadly died in 2009. He attended the

Glasgow School of Art and became the youngest artist to have his work hung in the Glasgow Art Galleries. I climbed several mountains with him, in particular Stuc a'Chroin covered in winter snow, with Robin sketching away, oblivious of the cold.

The Iona Community

The Iona Community was established by George Macleod who founded it in 1938. This community is an ecumenical group which seeks to tackle the problems and take the opportunities of communicating the Christian Gospel in today's world. Members spend a period of training at the Abbey before going out to serve as ministers, engineers, doctors, community workers, teachers and musicians, or as workers in other fields of work. They are particularly committed to working for peace and to serving in difficult places. The community is a leading influence in the recent Celtic Christian revival.

APPENDIX

Author's long-distance walks in the British Isles

1976	Lowestoft to St Davids
1977	Bromley to Steyning
1978	Bromley to Cornwall
1980	Barry to Llandudno
1981	Peterhead to Ardnamurchan Point
1982	Isle of Wight to Allendale Town
1983	Allendale Town to Durness
1984	Durness to Knoydart
1985	Galloway to Iona
1886	Outer Hebrides
1987	North Downs and South Downs Ways
1988	Orkney and Shetland
1990	Durness to Fort William
1991	Norfolk to the Fens
1997	Pembrokeshire Coastal Path

In 1995 I planned a walk from Lindisfarne (Holy Island) to Iona – a journey which, because of family commitments, never materialised. There is a St Cuthbert's Way between Lindisfarne and the Scottish Borders town of Melrose; the proposed, much longer journey would also be of considerable historical interest. The monastery of Lindisfarne was founded by the Irish monk Saint Aidan, who had been sent from Iona to Northumbria at the request of King Oswald *c*AD 635. It became the base for Christian evangelising in the North of England.

SOURCES AND BIBLIOGRAPHY

Ken Andrew, *The Southern Upland Way* (Western Section), HMSO (1984)

John Betjeman, *Collected Poems,* John Murray (1968)

Hamish Brown, *Hamish's Groats End Walk,* Gollantz, (1981)

Canadian Boat Song, The Oxford Book of English Verse, OUP, (1949)

P S Clarke, *Everymans Book of Saints,* Mowbray (1914)

Derek Cooper, *Road to the Isles,* Routledge and Kegan Paul, (1979)

Derek Cooper, *The Road to Mingulay,* A view of the Western Isles, Routledge & Kegan Paul plc (1985)

Dillan and Nora Chadwick, *The Celtic Realm,* Weidenfeld & Nicolson, (1967)

Michael and Jackie Cranefield, Bromley Baptist Church Outlook (Oct 1986)

The Gatliff Trust, *Report for the years 1985 to 1987,* Crofters' Hostels in the Outer Hebrides (1990)

John Hillaby, *Journey Through Britain,* Constable (1968)

Mark Douglas Home, *report,* The Independent (16 Mar 1987)

Hector Kyrne, *A Million and More Strides,* Robert Hale Ltd (1975)

Iris and Roger Legg, *The Colby Connection* (a family history) (1986)

D C Moir, *Scottish Hill Tracks,* Scottish Rights of Way Society (1995)

W H Murray, *The Islands of Western Scotland,* Eyre Methuen (1973)

W H Murray. *The Western Highlands of Scotland,* Companion Guides, (1985)

Peig Sayers (edited by S Ennis), *An Old Woman's Reflections,* Oxford University Press (1962)

New Shell Guide to Scotland, Editors Donald Macnie and Moray Mclaren (1977)

John Starkey, *The Road through the Isles,* Wildwood House (1986)

Frances Thomson, Harris and Lewis David and Charles (1987)

Wikipedia: Ailsa Craig, Baleshare Causeway, Cape Wrath lighthouse, The Iona Community, Kisimul Castle, Sandwood Bay, The Bridge to Nowhere, 1977/78 Whitbread Race.

ACKNOWLEDGMENTS

My special thanks goes to my late wife Iris for her love and support at 'Home Base'.

I am also grateful to Rev Roderick Mackinnon for the Gaelic translation of the 'Grace' and to Alison Graham for information on The Achiltibuie Garden Ltd (included in the End Notes).

During my expeditions I have experienced much kindness and hospitality from many people (some of whom are named) who helped me on the way: the British Isles are full of wonderful people – my indebtedness to you all!

Lastly a 'thank you' to my daughter Ruth for making many helpful suggestions regarding the text, to Lorna Coombs for her proof reading and to the staff of Xlibris for the design and layout of the book.

Lightning Source UK Ltd.
Milton Keynes UK
UKOW04f0613190216

268705UK00001B/84/P